W9-CXN-382

Praise for Two Breaths, One Step

"*Two Breaths, One Step* is a weave of extraordinary natural beauty, personal determination, intriguing cultural encounters, and magical spiritual moments— a significant personal odyssey coming together during a few months trekking the Himalayas. Sylvia writes with candor and the kind of descriptive detail that makes you feel you are walking right along with her."

—Joseph Selbie, author of *The Yugas*

"Rich with cultural, geographical, and personal details, Sylvia Verange's *Two Breaths, One Step* is a sensual encounter with the beauty and danger of the Himalayas. Like the artist she is, Verange paints a vivid picture of the sounds, smells, and the challenges of traveling in the highest mountains in the world."

—Nancy Anderson, author of *Work with Passion*

"Some journeys delve into the unknown, the exotic, and the new; Some journeys probe the past, into memories and lessons learned to find sensations long buried. Sylvia Verange's *Two Breaths, One Step* accomplishes both with grace, wit, and humor. A rare feat."

—Joseph Bharat Cornell, author of *The Sky and Earth Touched Me* and *Deep Nature Play*

HIKING ACROSS THE HIMALAYAS

Two Breaths, One Step

A VIREO BOOK | RARE BIRD BOOKS
LOS ANGELES, CALIF.

HIKING ACROSS THE HIMALAYAS

Two Breaths, One Step

Sylvia Verange

THIS IS A GENUINE VIREO BOOK

A Vireo Book | Rare Bird Books
453 South Spring Street, Suite 302
Los Angeles, CA 90013
rarebirdbooks.com

Copyright © 2018 by Sylvia Verange

FIRST TRADE PAPERBACK ORIGINAL EDITION

All rights reserved, including the right to reproduce this book or
portions thereof in any form whatsoever, including but not limited
to print, audio, and electronic. For more information, address:
A Vireo Book | Rare Bird Books Subsidiary Rights Department,
453 South Spring Street, Suite 302,
Los Angeles, CA 90013.

Photography and Artwork by Sylvia Verange

Set in Minion Pro
Printed in the United States.

10 9 8 7 6 5 4 3 2 1

Publisher's Cataloging-in-Publication data
Names: Verange, Sylvia, author.
Title: Two breaths, one step : hiking across the Himalayas /
Sylvia Verange.
Description: First Trade Paperback Original Edition |
A Vireo Book | New York, NY; Los Angeles, CA:
Rare Bird Books, 2018.
Identifiers: ISBN 9781945572890
Subjects: LCSH Verange, Sylvia—Travel—Nepal. | Verange,
Sylvia—Biography. | Hiking—Nepal. | Nepal—Description and
travel. | BISAC TRAVEL / Asia / India & South Asia | SPORTS &
RECREATION / Hiking
Classification: LCC DS493.53 .V47 2018 | DDC 915.496—dc23

For Dianthalin
who taught me the value of simplicity, beauty,
and truth, along with the love of travel.

Preface

THE INSPIRATION FOR THIS book came while hiking in Patagonia. As miles passed beneath my boots and wide-open skies stretched overhead, I found my thoughts drifting through numerous past adventures. For the next few months, my mind kept circling back to the memories, sights, sounds, and soul of the Himalayas, where I hiked over five hundred miles more than thirty years ago.

As with many good ideas, this one arose as I walked in nature. I rarely find that inspiration comes while sitting at a desk. Rather, that is where one slogs through the act of manifesting an idea into its physical form. I learned a long time ago that ideas just take a moment, while carrying them out may take years.

Prologue

IT WAS AFTER NINE when I began hiking up the valley from Pheriche. Details disappeared quickly as the fog and snow-laden clouds covered the land. The clouds blasted down the valley, and soon I stood in the middle of a snowstorm. Cold, cold, and more cold. I put on my rain pants, my jacket, and my vest, and soon I felt both hot and cold at the same time. As I crossed a turbulent river, I prayed not to slip or fall from the slick, snow-covered bridge. Before continuing up the next mountain, I made a brief stop for tea in a small house on the far side of the bridge.

As the trail climbed farther up the valley, the weather continued to deteriorate. I pushed on through the blizzard, the snow falling heavily around me, affording little visibility. The landscape quickly became a field of black and white, offering no clear distinctions or landmarks, the trail gone from view.

Soon, I noticed I could not see our Nepali guide, Dende, or anyone else. The world tightly closed around me, revealing only a few feet of visibility directly in front. The surrounding peaks of over twenty-six thousand feet remained tucked beneath a thick blanket of lofty white.

I called out Dende's name but no one answered, and I couldn't see anyone or anything through the blinding snowstorm.

I realized I was alone and the trail had completely disappeared. I had no idea where it was, nor did I know where I had ventured off from it. I was lost, and I had backpacked enough to know this was not a good sign, not a good sign at all. Below-freezing temperatures, a raging blizzard, no sign of the trail, few supplies with me (as most were with the porters), and the lateness of the afternoon compounded the situation. The thought of an evening alone in these conditions offered no comfort. I found shelter by crouching down behind a large boulder, which offered some relief from the heavy snow and fierce winds. I took out a small bag of cashews from my pack and tried to remain calm as I considered my options: stay put and hope someone would come looking for me, or move on—but in which direction? I decided to sit down and rest for a bit, until I could think more clearly and come up with a better plan.

The Sherpas carried both my tent and sleeping bag. When had I last seen them? It was unclear, and I didn't have a good sense of how much time had elapsed since. Every few minutes, I climbed out from behind the boulder and shouted Dende's name. As my cry was snatched by the wind, I retreated back behind the boulder. With the gales ripping around me, it seemed quite futile, but I didn't know what else to do. I looked at my watch. I'd been lost in the mountains before and I found it quite helpful to note the time, as it had a way of quickly becoming distorted when one was lost. Without the reference of a watch, I wouldn't know for sure if twenty minutes had passed, or one hour, or three hours.

After crouching behind the rock, coming out to shout every few minutes, and eating some nuts, my watch showed twenty minutes had passed. Then twenty-five, thirty. It required a supreme effort to remain calm. At last I heard an answer to my shouts, but I couldn't see anyone approaching in the white landscape. A speck of dark gray appeared farther down the slope and a lone figure slowly emerged out of the snowstorm. As I strained my eyes to see, I made out the form of Dende, a small smudge of a figure in the howling blizzard. I let out a sigh of relief, no longer alone.

The Opportunity

We find after years of struggle
that we do not take a trip; a trip takes us.
—Steinbeck, *Travels with Charley*

WE BEGAN WALKING WHERE the road ended.
In 1984, walking remained the only way
to reach most of the country. That meant walking
for days, weeks, or months, depending where one
wanted to go. I wanted to go to the high mountain
country of Nepal at the foot of the lofty peaks that
I could see rising in the distant sky. The journey
would extend over five hundred miles, walking
across the roof of the world, far more than I had
ever hiked before, and far more than I had ever
imagined hiking.

It really wasn't an "I" as four of us formed the
group. But I refer to "I" as most of the time I hiked
alone, unable to keep up with the other three who

lived or worked back home in the United States at elevations of 5,000 and 9,000 feet. I lived at about sea level, actually at an elevation of 115 feet, in a small town on the edge of the San Francisco Bay Area.

Although I knew the lush landscape around me would end in a matter of weeks, the bareness and desolation that lay ahead shocked me with its emptiness and stark beauty. The terraced hillsides, covered with small plots for growing the limited crops of the rising altitudes, reached toward the sky. The clear skies provided a perfect day for hiking toward the highest mountains of the world.

Inwardly I hoped the months of preparation for this adventure would prove adequate as I took my first step down the well-worn footpath. The paperwork, the lists of supplies, the packing, the leaving of the rest of my life in a state that it could be left: all of this melted away as I walked into the brilliant landscape of terraced rice fields climbing up the mountains, separated by ancient stone walls winding their way up the steep hills.

I felt a sense of relief as I left Kathmandu, the bustle of the growing city, the dust, the noise—the chaos a Westerner often feels in the cities of Asia. As the dusty bus pulled out of Kathmandu, the entire range of Himalayan peaks came into view. One incredible snow peak after another, a whole line of them rising far above the valley below. They seemed to extend forever as a sea of mountain peaks into the distance. A day or two earlier, the monsoons had ended and a vibrant, iridescent green color permeated the land. The rice terraces shimmered with an emerald-golden hue. Lush and verdant, they sparkled under the radiant sun.

The bus pulled out of Kathmandu at nine in the morning for the seven-hour ride to where the road ended in the small village of Jiri. Paul, Sidny, Peyton, our guide, five porters, and I boarded the vehicle for the usual noisy bus trip found in any developing country at that time. With mountains of gear strapped on top of the bus, many additional travelers sprawled across the numerous bags, baskets, and bundles secured above. It actually looked like it would be rather nice sitting atop the luggage piled high overhead, lumpy mounds that seemed to grow from the roof, the wind in your face as you gazed out at the gorgeous scenery. But Paul, the man who so generously agreed to let me tag along on this trip with him, had purchased us seats inside. He had paid for two seats for each of us so that we could travel in a bit more comfort. Even so, people, chickens, and bundles of what seemed like people's life's possessions completely surrounded us, smashing us between seas of bodies.

The seats in a Nepali bus were simply rough wood benches lined across the side of a center aisle. Each bench held four to six travelers in a space that held two passengers on a bus in the United States. Basically, folks would pile in and they didn't seem to mind squeezing yet another person in the row with their livestock and belongings spilling into the aisle. The hours passed slowly as the loud and raucous ride lasted most of the day.

We continued along a road filled with sharp hairpin turns; the bus was stuffy and cramped, and the heat suffocating as the windows did not open. As we passed an overturned truck, I remembered things could be very precarious on remote mountain roads. If anything happened, no help stood nearby— no highway patrol, no gas stations, no phones. We stopped for one delay after another, making the trip far longer than the quoted seven hours. Delays for roadwork, accidents, breakdowns of the bus, and both livestock and locals walking in the road added more hot and dusty hours to the trip.

The bus stopped for passengers to grab a quick lunch at one of the occasional food stands along the roadside. I was careful not to eat anything from which I might get sick. This ruled out about everything except the plain, wrapped packets of English biscuits that soon became one of my staples as I hiked across the mountains for the next few months. Finally, we crossed a visa check point, signed in, had our passports checked, and continued to our first destination, the small village of Kirantichap, at an elevation of 4,389 feet.

We spent the night at the Himalayan Hotel and Lodge, which sounds far grander than the reality. Three stories high, we stayed upstairs in the loft area with four basic wooden beds, a low ceiling, earthen floor, and a very shaky ladder for ascending and descending.

I arrived exhausted, famished, and with a pounding headache from the long bus trip. The hotelkeeper graciously prepared us tea along with an evening meal of rice and dahl, the traditional Nepali/Indian dish of cooked lentils. I immediately went to bed, but the stifling air prevented sleep, along with the numerous dogs screaming late into the night. At 5:00 a.m., I stumbled out of my sleeping bag. Although never a morning person, this quickly became the norm on this trip.

That first morning in late September 1984, I awoke with an upset stomach and piercing cramps. When my eyes caught the large red-stained area on the inside of my sleeping bag, I understood. My periods had never occurred regularly, sometimes seventeen days passed between them, and sometimes forty-two days. I stopped tracking my monthly cycles years ago, instead quietly awaiting their arrival.

Not knowing when my period would arrive created inconvenience at the best of times, and this was certainly not a welcomed sight the first morning of a long journey across an unknown landscape. I envied those women whose cycles arrived like clockwork: predictable to the day. They wouldn't have to clean up a mess like I now faced. With the barest of hygiene available, I began the chore of clean up. I climbed down the three flights of rough, wooden ladders and stairs with my sleeping bag bundled in my arms and walked to the small yard at the back of the lodge. I found a faucet off to the side and proceeded to wash my bag as best I could. I laid the down feather bag in the sun to dry while I went back upstairs to pack and see about breakfast. After two cups of black-spiced tea, sweetened with milk and generous amounts of sugar, I headed back to the trail for day two of the trek.

Paul had lived in Asia and decades earlier had trekked in Nepal. He felt more comfortable in the Hindu cultures of India and Nepal than the Muslim cultures of Pakistan, which also contained many of the world's highest peaks. Combined with his experience as a veteran ski patroller, he knew how to handle trekking in the mountains with us newbies in tow. He carefully planned the days so that we could acclimatize gradually to the high altitudes. Thus, we began hiking at the low altitudes, where the road ended, and chose not to fly directly to the higher elevations as most tourists did. We carefully followed the advice of seasoned mountaineers—climb high, sleep low, and spend a few weeks walking into the high altitudes giving our bodies time to adjust to the heights.

We immediately left Kathmandu the day the monsoons ended, hoping to get an advance start before the numerous expeditions of the trekking companies that would soon follow. We sought peace and solitude on the trail. As the companies planned their trips so far ahead and did not have the luxury to wait in Kathmandu for the rains to end, they had picked a date safely after the end of the monsoons. Also, if one waited two to three weeks after the monsoons ended, the land dried out—and most importantly, the leeches disappeared.

Although not as severe as the monsoons in Bangladesh, the monsoon in Nepal exerts a definite influence on the trekking season. Beginning in June, it rains almost every day until September, when the storms begin to recede. The plains and lower Himalayas receive more than 70 percent of their annual precipitation during the summer monsoon.

Even though the success of farming almost totally depends on the timely arrival of the summer monsoon, it periodically causes problems such as landslides and the subsequent loss of human lives, farmlands, and housing, as well as heavy flooding in the plains, not to mention great difficulty in the movement of goods and people. Conversely, when prolonged breaks in the summer monsoon occur, severe drought and famine often result.

The post-monsoon season usually begins with a slow withdrawal of the rains. This retreat leads to an almost complete disappearance of moist air by mid-October, and the accompanying disappearance of the leeches quickly follows. Since the trekking companies can be assured of cool, dry weather, mid-October marks the beginning of their expeditions to the high altitudes. While we were waiting in Kathmandu, the rains stopped one day, like a water faucet turning off. The following day we set out on our trek, which gave us about a three-week head start before many others hit the trails.

As we hiked along, I noticed how much I depended on Paul's judgment and skill, as well as his familiarity with both the landscape and the people of Nepal. He comfortably interacted with the Sherpas, and most importantly, he knew how to organize the logistics for such a trek once in Kathmandu.

I had met Paul a couple years earlier in Bend, a small town in eastern Oregon, while studying at the University of Oregon. At five foot six inches, his height blended in with that of the Nepali people. Though small in build and light in weight, Paul's body resembled steel, his muscles strong, taut, and lean. He worked on ski patrol at one of the big ski resorts in the west, Mt. Bachelor, just outside of Bend. His job as a ski patroller at 9,000 feet meant that he knew both first aid and mountain survival. Along with basic medical supplies, Paul brought suture supplies in case they would be useful on the trek to help with the medical needs of local villagers. He found many opportunities to administer to the locals, who quickly began to look on him as some type of god once word spread of Paul's skills and supplies. It seemed like magic to them that a small pill could make an illness or unwanted condition disappear. The requests for medical attention didn't cease as we progressed.

Paul's demeanor reflected a no-nonsense man: a person extremely disciplined and focused, straight as an arrow. Although others sometimes found his individual quirks annoying or comical, I truly admired his dedication and numerous accomplishments, along with his patience with those less knowledgeable than he. Paul had lived in India for one and a half years, and though he had trekked in Nepal before, he had never visited the Solu-Kumba, also known as the Everest Region. We headed for Everest Base Camp, our destination situated at an elevation of over eighteen thousand feet.

A three-hour drive from the University of Oregon, Mt. Bachelor Ski Resort sat within the Cascade Mountains, between the high desert landscapes of eastern Oregon and the lush valleys of the western slopes. For several years, I skied directly behind Paul as he patrolled the runs. Following closely behind him provided me with excellent training, and my skiing skills quickly improved. When he turned, I turned, and thus we skied the mountain the entire day. We would stop briefly for lunch, and Paul would unpack a series of small, stainless steel food containers filled with cashew nuts, fruit, lentils, and perhaps a few other items. Paul ate a basic diet; with sugar and fat scarce, if ever present. He used to remark on how fast someone would change their diet once they suffered a heart attack. He had seen plenty of these over the years, and I knew there existed little chance of Paul experiencing one. I recently heard that at eighty-nine years young, he still works full-time patrolling yet another mountain ski resort in the western United States.

Paul's clear blue eyes spoke volumes about his dedication and discipline. His life centered on patrolling, and the rest of the time he could be found meditating, a practice he had pursued for decades. He lived simply and his needs were basic. Unwavering in his commitments and emotionally strong, Paul could be intense and unnerving. Like a tree, he knew how to bend so he wouldn't break, and I greatly admired this about Paul. His age of almost thirty years my senior gave him both insights and experience I respected.

Amazingly, once I got to know Paul, I discovered that we shared a unique background. He had produced films in Hollywood for ten years and thus he knew the movie industry of my youth. He had worked on the television series *Gunsmoke, Have Gun—Will Travel*, and *How The West Was Won*, among many others. Paul had worked alongside Lee Marvin, James Arness, and Peter Graves, all important names from my childhood.

∾

I GREW UP IN Pacific Palisades, a secluded area of Los Angeles between the sleepy town of Santa Monica and the coastal enclave of Malibu. Pacific Palisades had long attracted actors from the film industry with its proximity to Hollywood, as it continues to do today. But the 1950s existed as a very different time and place than today, a time when actors did not necessarily live in mansions, nor did they make exorbitant amounts of money. I grew up with their names and families close at hand, and we thought of them as just the folks next door. Not until I was older did I realize that not everyone grew up with such an amazing cast of characters.

James Arness starred in *Gunsmoke*, the longest-running prime time drama series in US television history by the end of its twenty-year run in 1975. He and his family lived two doors down from our family in Rustic Canyon, a wooded section of Pacific Palisades. His daughter Jenny and my older sister palled around together as childhood buddies. When my mother planned a summer vacation for herself and my oldest sister, my mother invited Jenny to accompany them while I and Christina, the two younger children, went to Girl Scout Camp. It would be our turn to travel later. The tragic death of Jenny in 1975, and her mother's death the following year, left vast holes of emptiness in our community. James Arness's younger brother, Peter Graves, also lived close by, and his daughter Claudia was Christina's age—Christina being my other sister, just one year older than I.

Lee Marvin, who occasionally worked on the same sets as Paul, lived down the street, and his daughter Courtenay was also Christina's age. Other families with young, school-age children who were school buddies of either me or my sisters included the Serlings (creator of *The Twilight Zone* with daughter Nan), Jerry Paris (*The Dick Van Dyke Show* with daughter Julie), Alfred Newman (Hollywood film score composer with sons Tommy and David), and Ted Cassidy (the actor who played Lurch in *The Addams Family*). As a child, I enjoyed catching a glimpse of Ted as he came out the front door and picked up the morning paper, his immense height of six foot nine stooping to clear the door frame. And over the back fence lived Richard Maibaum, best known for his screenplay adaptations of Ian Fleming's classic *James Bond*, and Berni Gould, writer for *Let's Make a Deal*, whose daughter, Abby, who still remains Christina's best childhood friend.

During the filming of *Have Gun—Will Travel*, Paul discovered Eastern Oregon, as many of the sets centered around the small town of Sisters and the open desert between Sisters and Bend. When it came time for him to leave the hustle and bustle of Hollywood, he chose to make Bend his home.

The other two hikers along on the expedition with Paul and me were Sidny and Peyton, both from Bend, Oregon, as well. They didn't know Paul well, but they had heard that he planned a trekking trip to Nepal and wanted to join the expedition. When others expressed interest, Paul responded with generosity. If someone wanted to go on the adventure, he figured there must be a reason for them to go. Thus, he had also taken newbies like us on previous expeditions.

Sidny and Peyton both worked at the local hospital in Bend, Sidny as an emergency room nurse and Peyton as an X-ray technician. I didn't know either of them; our first meeting was not to occur until we met up in Kathmandu, several months down the road.

∾

FOR ME, THE TRIP began earlier that year in the foothills of the Sierra Nevada Mountains of California. Shortly after finishing college, I moved to the Sierras to sort out the next stage of my life. I stayed in a tiny cabin close to the small house of my sister and her husband. Their lives revolved around their work, and they were 100 percent focused on the direction they wanted their lives to go. In contrast to the unshakable bedrock on which they stood, I found myself confused and anxious, still trying to find my way forward.

Even though I had recently graduated from college with an employable skill, I felt something lacking in my life. The time between college and figuring out what to do with the rest of my life created distress for me. Sometimes I thought I came into the world with a large dose of self-doubt that held me back, or even worse, paralyzed me from taking action. Even though others found me courageous, I often felt terrified, forcing myself to just jump in and walk through the fear.

After almost burning down my sister and brother-in-law's rustic cabin, I needed to find another place to live. As a result of this incident, my relationship with my sister became rather prickly. My sister exhibited a lot of anger as a child, but by early adulthood, it had run its course and had mostly dissipated, which I always thought a great blessing. It was as though the anger had simply burned up like a chemical reaction, leaving a clean, polished empty slate upon which it rarely, if ever, surfaced again.

I lacked the most basic fire-building skills, as my outdoor experience consisted of backpacking in the high country, where campfires were prohibited. When I felt cold on backpacking trips, I would put on an extra layer of clothing or retreat into my sleeping bag for warmth. For cooking, a light-weight backpacking stove sufficed. And growing up in the suburbs, I knew nothing about the details of chopping wood or building a fire.

While trying to create a fire in the cabin's wood stove, I neglected to notice that the stove pipe rising to the ceiling somehow dislodged itself, and rather than escaping to the outside through the vent, the smoke poured directly onto the wood ceiling. There was no water in the cabin, and not knowing what else to do, I ran for help.

After that fiasco, I left my residence at my sister's cabin and stayed briefly at a friend's house until I found a place for rent farther down the country dirt road. A rough shell of an unfinished house sat squarely on the top of a ridge, looking out to the eastern hills. The house became available for rent because the young couple building the house ran out of money and returned to the city to work so they could continue to fund their dream.

The living space consisted of one main room with a small wooden table and two wooden chairs, a sleeping alcove off to one side, a make-shift kitchen, and a halfway-finished bathroom. I carried in my own drinking water as a deep, rich, brownish, red-hued liquid, rich in iron, flowed from the taps, identical to the color of the land outside. I don't remember any heat, but as spring became summer, heat no longer mattered. I soon discovered several additional reasons for the very inexpensive rent.

The unfinished state of the house left many small cracks and openings visible to the outside world. Open spaces occurred around window and doorframes, as well as between the wooden boards of the framework. This meant air, as well as other things, could enter easily. Shortly after moving in, I noticed a bump on my right thigh. I assumed a mosquito had bitten me and I didn't give it much attention. A day or two later, I went for a run in the surrounding hills. I had established a training program of running at least thirty miles each week, a routine that later proved totally inadequate for the expedition. A week into the trek, I realized I lacked the preparation for the emotional and psychological stress that accompanied the exhaustive physical demands of the trip, despite both my training and previous travels in developing countries.

The morning I went for a run, I suddenly lost my balance, fell on the dirt trail, and twisted my ankle.

I thought I sprained my ankle because the trail was so uneven and perhaps my attention wandered. But a couple of days later, the "mosquito bite" that appeared on my right thigh turned black and a large red ring appeared around it, about an inch out from the bite's center. Clearly not a mosquito bite, I visited the local medical clinic located on the ridge. The doctor on duty that day gave me antibiotics and told me if I didn't see improvement in a couple of days, give him a call.

The next morning I could barely get out of bed as a lump the size of a golf ball appeared on my right groin. The mosquito bite began to cave in on itself, forming a black hole in my right thigh. With the worsening condition of my leg, I became alarmed. I called the clinic and a different doctor answered my call. I mentioned my previous visit and the appearance of the large lump.

Next, the conversation went something like this:

The doctor: "Is there a red ring around the bump?"

Me: "Yes, but it's more like a black hole."

Doctor: "It's black?"

Me: "Yes."

My anxiety level rose steadily. The doctor continued, "Can you come in right away?"

I dropped everything and headed back to the clinic.

Fortunately, the doctor on duty knew of this type of condition. He told me an assassin bug, the third most poisonous insect in the United States, had bitten me. The bug lived in a symbiotic relationship with the wood rat. The poison affected the central nervous system, which explained why

I had felt off balance during the run, fallen down, and subsequently sprained my ankle.

The doctor prescribed steroids and the situation immediately improved. I returned home feeling vulnerable, knowing the lack of separation between the inside and the outside of the house did not provide a barrier to the many animals and insects surrounding me. Asleep in my own bed, in this flimsy house, a poisonous insect had bitten me.

∾

THAT WINTER, I TRAVELED to Bend for a ski vacation. One day Paul mentioned his upcoming plans to trek in Nepal. I instantly knew that I was going on the trip, although how it was going to happen remained a mystery. I had backpacked before, with eight days being the longest trip I had completed and that one in the mountains of California many years earlier.

Previously, I hiked to eight or nine thousand feet, no higher. I vividly recall Paul's comment when I said I wanted to go with him to Nepal. He told me we would be in very remote areas and not near any services or medical support. If something happened and I needed medical attention, the only way out, other than walking, consisted of airlift by helicopter. The cost: 2,000 bucks (in 1984 dollars)—credit cards not accepted.

Paul calmly continued with, "Are you comfortable with that?"

I considered this for about three seconds, and I heard myself say, "Yes, I'm comfortable with that." Although I did not understand or absorb the full impact of my response, a green light brightly flashed and I set my sights on the Himalayas.

My savings consisted of a few thousand dollars, enough for a cheap trip to Asia. I had earned money since the age of thirteen and developed a strong habit of saving over the years. Early jobs as a babysitter transformed into housecleaner, waitress, store clerk, and various entrepreneurial projects. In our family, it was understood that we needed to work for "extras," including cameras, skiing equipment and ski trips, or any other luxury. Unlike the mother of one of my school friends, my mother didn't think it was fair that children should have to pay for dental care or other necessities. Thus, the basics were covered.

My mother carefully managed finances and provided for our needs. A few years before my birth, my father built our house for $5,000, originally as a spec house. Upon completion, mother liked it so much that they decided to live in the house and moved on to build other houses in the neighborhood. Six months before his death, my father took out an additional life insurance policy, even though no sign of illness existed. Mother wisely saved the money to cover the cost of college for us three girls. Our lifestyle did not require a lot of money. With the house paid for, no mortgage existed. We ate at home, sewed most of our clothes, and enjoyed long hours outdoors or doing creative projects for fun.

Raised with a strong sense of independence, I was given a lot of latitude without many, if any, restrictions. Left to fill my own time with projects, I wasn't asked as to my whereabouts or when I would return home. Even though my father died when I was three years old, my mother provided a stable environment for us. Mother was more lenient, and she often told me that my life would have been very different if my father had lived. He was Italian and his folks were from the "old world," which clearly meant more formal and strict character traits. Unable to articulate or understand the loss of my father at such a young age, I moved on to the business of growing up. A friend of mine once commented that rather than getting over the loss of a parent at a young age, one gets through it. Perhaps losing a father is like losing an arm; one never gets it back, but one learns to live without it.

When I turned eighteen, I went to court to receive the $13,000 that had grown from my portion of my father's life insurance policy: not enough for a four-year private university, but enough for an education at UC Berkeley. Fortunately, I loved learning and I excelled at school. This made it possible to receive several grants that did not require repayment. Combined with summer jobs between the years of university studying, I built up a small savings account that I tapped into for the Himalayan adventure.

∾

I HAVE OFTEN BEEN called to places by the sound of a name: Zanzibar, Kathmandu, Gokyo, Sulawesi, and Bukkatingi. The list continues: Kigali, Ura, Tiger's Nest, Ushuaia, and many more. I rarely have any specific or tangible idea about the place, but for some reason the names pull me toward them. Something about the sound of certain places invites me, the way the words fall off the tongue creating a sense of mystery. Kathmandu was such a name. It invoked something exotic, something remote and out of the ordinary. Perhaps, like me, others remain helpless before the strong magnetic pull that ceaselessly ropes them in, like a fish drawn in by the mesmerizing allure of a winged insect darting across the sun-drenched surface of a languid mountain stream. Names continue to attract me as the list unfolds: Botswana, Iguazu, Rishikesh…

I had traveled to developing countries before, but not to Asia. Years earlier I traveled for a year on a shoestring budget through Mexico and Central America, continuing through South America to Brazil. I spoke enough Spanish that I was able to communicate, although for the most part the locals spoke only the indigenous dialects in the remote areas through which I traveled.

Asia was different. Mysterious and intriguing, the Himalayas had attracted me since childhood. I remember watching the television accounts of Lowell Thomas Sr. and his son Lowell Thomas Jr.'s amazing journey to Tibet in 1949. The Tibetan government invited them to make a film with the hope that their reports would help persuade the US government to defend Tibet against the Chinese. The trip lasted four hundred days, the father and son team the last Westerners to reach Lhasa before the Chinese invaded in 1951.

CBS did not broadcast the resultant film, *Expedition to Lhasa, Tibet,* until years later, but the Thomas's book about the expedition, *Out of This World,* published in 1950, became an immediate bestseller. In the 1950s, CBS produced the travelogue special television series *High Adventure*. Recording the Thomas's journeys to the far corners of the world, the series included their amazing adventures in Tibet as some of the first westerners to enter the country in centuries.

My love of travel and my love for independence came from my mother. She loved to travel, and growing up foreign students often stayed at our house for a weekend or longer. This gave me an early understanding and deep appreciation of other cultures, and I developed my mother's fascination with far away exotic lands. Many years later, after my mother had passed away, I traveled to Bhutan. I remember my brother-in-law remarking that mother would have loved to know that I was going to Bhutan, visiting a place she had spoken of long ago.

Through the foreign students, I began to observe that other people did things differently than we did: they dressed differently, spoke differently, and had very different customs. This formed the groundwork for the development of an inclusive and welcoming interest in others, leading to a lifelong curiosity of our diversity as humans. Later, in my adult years, I noticed that people who had served in the Peace Corps were often more open minded and accepting than others, especially in sharp contrast with the perceived American luxury of being able to live in relative isolation from the rest of the world.

Mother loved anything Latin, and I remember the car radio playing Spanish music as we drove around town picking up groceries, getting gas, or running errands. Mother didn't speak Spanish, but the Latin culture spoke to her. However, the sounds of rock and roll that played endlessly on the radio enthralled me. I vividly remember listening to the latest pop songs on the radio as Mom and I drove to town, and after a short time, mother would simply say, "That's long enough," as she turned the radio dial to a station with music more to her liking. In hindsight, what a gift it could have been to practice more patience and to be more cognizant of others' feelings; a missed opportunity to practice compassion for others' needs over my own, especially on unimportant things that seemed so important at the time.

Perhaps my half-brother's participation in the World Olympic Games of Tokyo in 1964 triggered my mother's interest in Asia. She left us with a caretaker and went to Japan for six weeks to watch my half-brother take part in the bicycle races. After that, we started having foreign students— mostly from Japan—stay at our house during their university studies at UCLA.

My half-brother raced throughout the world, leaving the United States when I was eight or nine years old and returning with a Brazilian wife and child about seven years later. We didn't know each other well, given that he was sixteen years my senior and had lived abroad for much of my childhood. The gap between us loomed too large, and we never reconnected as I soon embarked for college and pursued my own path.

In my childhood home, an immensely long shelf extended the entire length of the living room. Proudly displayed along the top of the shelf, far too many trophies to count stood firmly from one end to the other, remembrances of the numerous races my brother had won. The tallest trophy stood in the center with the others descending in height out to the far ends of the shelf, creating a symmetrically balanced display. Years later, my half-brother went on to set several national bicycle records, as well as securing a place in the Mountain Bike Hall of Fame as one of the first inventors of the mountain bike, The Topanga, named after his beloved canyon in the Santa Monica Mountains. He was also inducted to the Road Bike Hall of Fame for his numerous records and awards in that sport.

Mother managed her budget carefully, making sure to put aside money for travel. As a child, my sister Christina and I reaped the benefits of two wonderful trips to foreign countries, and the allure of travel continued over the years. After college, I toyed with the idea of going to Asia, particularly the area of Srinagar in northern India, but that area remained off limits with war and conflict breaking out across the region. With Paul's trip in the planning stages, the Himalayas reeled me in like a fish lured by sparkling bait hitting the glassy surface of a summer lake.

The Preparation

Whatever you can do, or dream you can, begin it.
Boldness has genius, power, and magic to it.
—Goethe

As the spring of 1984 wore on, a growing pile of camping equipment began to accumulate on the floor of the main room in the unfinished house. The pile included an orange insulating sleeping pad, down sleeping bag, tent, canteen, two sets of long underwear, down jacket with hood, rain jacket, rain pants, hiking boots and socks, iodine crystals to purify the water (a method I had used for years), malaria pills, and so forth. Additionally, I purchased an updated version of the first trekking guidebook to Nepal, published in 1972. I created numerous lists of supplies, medicine, necessary shots, dates for visas, passport updates, and hundreds of other necessities required in planning a trip to a remote area where supplies were not available. Fortunately, with my early independence, I had developed a strong sense of planning that I knew was essential in accomplishing any goal.

Cold weather clothes only. No hiking pants or hiking shorts lay in the pile. If I didn't want the locals to think of me as a prostitute, better to hike in a long skirt, my legs covered. Like most places of the world, today the trails of Nepal fill with Westerners wearing all manner of clothing, usually dressed in the latest high-tech hiking gear with the associated electronic accoutrements. But in 1984, none of that modern gear existed.

This resonated with me as I preferred not standing out, and I tended to dress conservatively whenever traveling, especially in developing countries. To this day, I prefer to keep a low profile, far easier to accomplish by wearing simple, well-worn clothes, with perhaps a good set for border crossings and such.

In addition, among the petite Nepali people, my calves would stand out. As a child with large and muscular calves, strangers used to stop my sister and I to ask if we were ballet dancers. Today my calves remain the same size as at age nine. I went through my teenage years and early adult life feeling uncomfortable about my legs. I wanted the thin calves of a movie star actress, and not until years later did I appreciate receiving compliments on my shapely calves. The few times one of the Nepali porters caught a glimpse of my calves, they stared wide-eyed, the size of my calves huge in comparison to theirs. I found it best to keep them covered underneath a long skirt.

Gore-Tex had just hit the consumer market, and I splurged on a pair of North Face, navy-blue, Gore-Tex shell pants for one hundred dollars. I skimped on the rain jacket, opting for a royal-blue shell from the outdoor store REI, which quickly became a key article on the trip and a great buy at twenty-five dollars. I purchased lightweight Nike high tops made with more fabric than the heavier leather hiking boots of the early 1970s. Without the availability of Gore-Tex boots, I protected them the old-fashioned way: generously applying a greasy, waxy water sealant, heating the wax with a hairdryer, and then vigorously rubbing the melted wax deeply into the material.

Although teahouses rented spaces for sleeping, I planned to sleep in a tent to avoid the thick, smoky homes of the villagers. We also knew that the houses could get quite crowded once the trekking season got in full swing. In the layout of a rural Nepali home, the earthen floor surrounded a cooking area and the home filled with smoke. As I would spend close to three months in the tent, I knew I wanted a tent in which I could sit upright. I purchased a dome tent from REI, set it up in the yard, along with the rain fly, and sealed the seams, making it waterproof.

I also purchased a large, cheap army surplus duffle bag to hold everything. The Sherpas slung a wide, woven strap called a tumpline over their heads, resting it on their foreheads. The strap fell across their backs, supporting impossible loads. With their loads piled high above their heads and their two small legs reaching to the ground, the Sherpas usually walked barefoot along the trails. All one saw from the back were two small legs carrying outrageously heavy loads up very steep mountain paths. Sherpas with multiple sheets of glass strapped to their backs, five and six foot boards of lumber extending far above their heads, weights on their backs that I could not imagine carrying. Essentials needed by the villagers were carried in one step at a time, including building supplies, food that was not grown locally, and all household necessities.

Today, Sherpas carry Western-style packs legally limited to specified weight amounts. In 1984, no regulations existed restricting the loads Sherpas could carry. I carried a small pack filled with the day's provisions, including warm clothes, rain gear, food, water, my camera, and anything else I deemed necessary, as the supplies with the Sherpas remained unavailable until we set up camp each night. We purchased other specific materials with our guide before leaving Kathmandu. As the departure day approached, I began stuffing the supplies into the duffle, and the weight and size of the growing duffle shocked me.

I decided to purchase the necessary air tickets as I went along, thinking it would be less expensive and give me more flexibility. I learned from earlier adventures that the best information on cheap flights could be gained by talking with other travelers once the trip had begun. Thus, for the first leg of the trip, I bought a ticket from San Francisco to Amsterdam, planning to visit a college friend who lived in Holland.

Once in Amsterdam, I found a cheap ticket to Kathmandu via Bombay, India, on Aeroflot Airlines. I quickly understood why the airline priced the ticket so inexpensively. In the 1980s, Aeroflot was known for not arriving at their destinations. The plane I boarded in Amsterdam for Kathmandu, via Bombay, never made it to Nepal. After Bombay, the plane landed in Dhaka, the capital of Bangladesh, considerably east of our goal of Kathmandu.

As the plane descended, I wondered where we would land as most of the ground below us disappeared under acres of water. With the monsoons at their peak, one-third of the entire country of Bangladesh lay submerged beneath water. With the rain falling down in sheets, the air hot and humid, the plane descended.

Once we landed, I saw a large billboard proudly displaying the following message:

"See Bangladesh Before the Tourists Do."

A bus shuttled me and the other plane passengers from the airport to a nearby hotel, where we remained sequestered for one night. As we crossed the street to the hotel, I felt like a caged animal. The streets filled with the people of Bangladesh, everyone's eyes focused on us, the only whites in sight. Everyone crowded around us and stared. We must have been the first foreign tourists to enter the country—perhaps an occasional businessperson visited, but certainly no tourists.

Before the plane landed in Bombay, I had begun to feel physically uncomfortable, and I had asked if there was a doctor on board. No doctor responded to my request and the plane continued on its journey. By the time the plane set down in Dhaka, my skin itched, my entire body gnawing at me in distress.

At the hotel in Dhaka, I again requested to see a doctor, and after several hours a doctor arrived. I felt scared and nervous. I questioned the doctor's skill, though given we did not share a common language, communication remained severely limited. I received medication and continued to wait, along with the other passengers, for someone to tell us what lay ahead. The night passed fairly quietly in the hotel, with a simple evening meal provided for us. The staff asked us not to leave the hotel, which wasn't an option as they had taken our passports. The next morning, we eventually returned to the airport, and after various delays, our plane headed for Kathmandu.

By the time I arrived in Kathmandu, my hair had begun falling out and my entire body had begun peeling. Even the skin on my stomach and the palms of my hands was falling away. I heard about a Western clinic, and I headed in that direction to sort out the cause of these symptoms.

I learned that my body had developed an allergic reaction to the malaria medication prescribed for me before I left California. The new doctor prescribed another round of medicine and said I must wait for the malaria medication to work itself through my body, a process of several weeks.

This was not the last time malaria prevention medicine complicated my life and demanded my full attention. Years later, shortly after arriving in Africa, I discovered that the malaria prevention pills prescribed by my doctor were useless in Africa. They worked for mosquitos in Asia, but in Africa the mosquitos just loved them, attracted to the body like candy. In the United States, I purchased a handful of pills for about eighty dollars. When I purchased the same number of correct pills in Africa, I paid $2.79.

Fortunately, the monsoons continued preventing us from beginning the trek. But I couldn't do anything other than rest, physically exhausted from the poison circulating in my body. I headed back to the hotel and slept for days. Eventually, I woke up and wandered into town in search of food.

I walked the few blocks to the main dusty street of Kathmandu. The large array of Western foods surprised me, everything from lasagna to bagels with cream cheese to rich chocolate cake. This incredible variety resulted from the long tradition of mountaineers arriving in Kathmandu from all corners of the world to organize expeditions into the Himalayas. Budget travelers knew Kathmandu as an oasis of delicious food, especially if one craved a dish from his home country.

I settled on a small restaurant and ordered soup. As I sat at the table eating my soup, I overheard a conversation at the next table. An older British man sitting at the table next to me spoke of medical treatments. His hand held a small glass bottle containing very thin silver needles, about two inches in length. My ears perked up as I heard the word "acupuncture." Familiar with acupuncture, I had tried it years earlier for difficulties with headaches. In the mid 1970s, acupuncture remained under the radar, not yet legal in California. I remembered calling a practitioner in San Francisco, strictly coached beforehand not to mention the word "acupuncture" on the phone. Our phone conversation consisted of a set of codes I followed in order to schedule an appointment with the acupuncturist.

The results of the treatments impressed me and I thought perhaps this British man, sitting near me in the cafe in Kathmandu, might be able to help. I gathered my energy and went over and introduced myself, asking if he thought acupuncture could improve my condition.

He said the malaria medication acted as a poison and set up an allergic reaction. He continued, saying the acupuncture treatments would speed up the process, moving the poison more quickly through my body. After I expressed a willingness to try, the doctor, Julian, agreed to begin treatments the next day at my hotel.

Months later, upon my return to the States, I learned the malaria medication prescribed by my doctor had resulted in so many side effects that

European governments had banned the drug over ten years earlier. Once back in California, I made an appointment with my doctor, who was clearly embarrassed by his lack of knowledge on the subject and sincerely apologized for his mistake.

I spent the next few days in Kathmandu receiving acupuncture treatments from Julian and resting. The day the rains stopped, I knew it would be time to leave the city and begin hiking. I needed to build up my strength for the long trek that lay ahead. Upon arriving, I checked into the Kathmandu Guest House, and the following day I moved to the Star Hotel, costing only 28 rupees— or about $1.50/night—instead of the 78 rupees at the Guest House. Although I preferred the Kathmandu Guest House, I was keen to save money to stretch my modest budget. While I rested at the hotel, Paul, Sidny, and Peyton busied themselves with exploring Kathmandu and the surrounding villages, all of us waiting for the skies to clear.

In between my resting and their sightseeing, we shopped for supplies, and another pile of gear began to grow on the floor of the hotel room. We purchased about two days worth of food to take with us, as a safety precaution should we not find enough food on the trail. Our plan consisted of buying most of what we needed along the way, which meant that upon our arrival at a village, one of the porters would scout in search of a villager with food to sell—usually potatoes—and if we were lucky, perhaps something green, maybe chard or spinach. The lack of meat didn't bother me, as for years I had preferred vegetarian food.

The food we purchased in Kathmandu included:

- 2 nonfat milk bags
- 2 bags of tea
- 1 kg of sugar
- 3 kg of rice
- 5 kg of noodles
- 3 kg flour
- 5 bags muesli
- 5 bags wheat
- 2 kg dhal
- spices of chile, curry, pepper, turmeric, and salt
- 12 kg cashews
- 6 kg raisins
- 2 kg yellow raisins
- 4 jars of jam
- 4 jars of peanut butter

We also bought enough bread and cheese for several days, until we could find the next village bakery en route. Other supplies we purchased included:

- 1 flashlight
- 5 spare bulbs
- 4 umbrellas (We followed the tradition of hiking with an umbrella for sun protection at the lower altitudes, and it turned out to be a great idea.)
- cooking supplies for the porters, including various pots and bowls
- 12 candles
- 2 wash cloths
- 1 bag washing powder
- 3 pots with lids
- 5 plates, cups, and spoons
- one 5 gal plastic container for a water bottle
- 1 bottle for oil
- potato peeler
- knife
- 2 plastic buckets for water
- washing bowl
- 10-liter bottle for kerosene
- 6 pairs of Chinese sneakers for the porters (We decided on this extra purchase because the porters generally hiked barefoot, since they didn't own shoes. Although not of great quality, the Chinese tennis shoes were better than nothing.)
- 2 baskets

After each shopping trip, we piled the supplies into a rickshaw for the ride back to the hotel and divided them into smaller piles for each of us to add to our already heavy packs.

Toward the Sky

Let silence take you to the core of life.

—Rumi

AFTER THE NINE-HOUR BUS trip from Kathmandu, and a night in the village of Kirantichap, we began our hike toward Everest Base Camp. The trek would cover about 350 miles round trip and we expected to be gone approximately 35 days, climbing 35,000 feet and descending 25,000 feet just in the process of getting to Base Camp at 18,000 feet. The high ascent and descent resulted from the fact that the trail continually wound up one mountain and down another, rather than the steady incline and decline more common when hiking the California Sierra Nevadas. I would need to cross a sea of mountains before reaching Base Camp.

That first full day, we hiked nine miles to the village of Yarsa, at an elevation of 6,474 feet. I hiked in a skirt and shirt tailored from a tiny shop in Kathmandu, quickly realizing a skirt provided a much more comfortable hiking option than pants. Before beginning the trek, I had walked into a small shop on one of the hidden, dusty lanes in Kathmandu. Inside I spotted an old pedal sewing machine, a beautifully made Singer like the one at my childhood home, the sewing machine on which I learned to sew at age nine. The machine folded nicely inside the top wooden area, making a flat table top when not in use. My sister still uses that same machine, having never made the transition to a more modern electric machine—certainly a less beautifully crafted sewing machine.

Growing up, I loved visiting the fabric store in our small town. It was owned by an elderly Eastern European immigrant, a not-too-friendly, tall, thin man with white disheveled hair, wearing a gray rumpled suit. The store stretched lengthwise from front to back, with a narrow street front. Colorful bolts of fabric rose from the floor toward the ceiling. Stools standing at the back counter displayed various pattern books with the names of *McCall*, *Vogue*, and *Simplicity* boldly splashed across their covers. I used each of these patterns and sometimes I created my own, copying from an article of clothing I bought in a store—or more likely, borrowed from a friend.

I, along with my sister, enjoyed sewing most of our clothes and other necessities. Each summer we made large beach towels, purchasing brightly printed terry cloth material and neatly hemming the edges.

I particularly loved gazing at the racks of ribbons against one wall. Ribbons of numerous colors and widths: embroidered ones, plain ones, fancy ones. Ribbons of velvet, grosgrain, moray, and so many other materials. Sometimes, I would design a dress beginning with a particular ribbon as a decorative touch, and the dress would be a backdrop for the lovely ribbon. In the school days of my youth, we wore dresses or skirts; no pants were allowed until well into my high school years. The bathroom drawers held a large collection of colorful ribbons, worn in my long, brown hair when pulled tightly back in a ponytail or wrapped in a bun.

My older sister taught me to sew on the Singer pedal machine, and I completed my first skirt, a bright-green-colored paisley print, at age nine. For the next ten years, yards of fabric covered the living room floor, tissue paper patterns carefully pinned across the carpet. Mother checked the layout before I made a cut, ensuring one-way patterns and the nap of fabrics, like corduroy and velvet, went the right direction. Sometimes a pin or two lay buried within the carpet, later discovered by someone's bare foot, or hopefully by the weekly vacuuming, which was part of our regular house chores.

Before I learned to sew on the machine, I spent countless hours fashioning clothes for my Barbie doll. With so many fabric remnants around the house, we didn't consider purchasing store made outfits; rather, we loved creating our own crafted garments. Before we learned the intricacies of creating machine-made buttonholes, we dressed our Barbies in handmade plaid skirts and shirts with simple snap closures down the back. Although the outfits were not fancy in design or style, our vivid imaginations supplied the rest. It was like having a wonderful sheet of crisp white blank paper. We were free to create whatever clothes designs we wanted. This nurtured our sense of creativity and entrepreneurship as we were responsible for the results rather than receiving the immediate gratification a store purchase would provide.

My sister and I created various sorts of sewing projects. Each year, after Christmas, we patiently collected the pine needles from the fir tree and filled hand-sewn sachet bags that we fashioned out of satin, lace, and other fabric remnants. The smell from the pine needles lasted forever, and many of the sachets still dangle from hangers in my closet or lay hidden among layers of clothing in the chest of drawers.

We made bookmarks using a strip of rawhide topped with two circles of brightly colored felt, handsewn together around the edge with a decorative button-hole stitch. For small Christmas gifts we crafted many of these, using red felt on one side and a rich forest green on the other. On top of the circle, we embroidered the initials of the person who was to receive the gift. Our projects expanded in junior high school as girls took sewing and cooking classes, while boys enrolled in wood and machine shop.

My sister Christina created a very successful entrepreneurial project making purses. She discovered an exclusive leather store in Beverly Hills, specializing in making custom coats and jackets. They filled bags with small remnants left over from their production. The storeowners had no use for the scraps and threw bags of them out with the weekly trash. Christina made regular trips to the store, returning with garbage-size bags of colorful scraps. Colors of white, black, dark brown, light brown, taupe, and rust in both leather and suede filled the bags. My sister spent hours producing small purses with fringe hanging from the bottom, creating an immediate local success in the late sixties and early seventies. Christina thrived from her lasting sales at the local consignment store, Pots of Gold.

Because my creations were more labor intensive and not as commercially viable, they did not meet with immediate commercial success. Our projects kept us busy as we got older because we wanted spending money for our growing interests, such as skiing and photography.

While in high school, I studied fabric designing and fabric dyeing at UCLA, learning to work with exquisite silks, linens, and wools, boiling buckets of material over the kitchen stove, mother relentlessly patient as I explored yet another creative endeavor.

I filled large notebooks with test samples of fabrics, noting the different combinations I assembled of dye, water, and technique, often creating magical results. These notebooks remain in my home, in some forgotten cupboard along with other childhood memories. My love of fabrics followed me as I matured. I still find myself picking up gorgeous fabrics from the far corners of the world, and I more often than not purchase more than I can handle.

Once I found the small tailor's shop in Kathmandu, I picked out colorful, blue, cotton-stripped material that I didn't think would easily show dirt. I requested the tailor copy the shirt and skirt I wore into the shop. The shop owner, a Nepali woman, told me to come back the next day.

I returned and paid the bill of less than four dollars, realizing the next time I traveled to Nepal it would be better to arrive without any extra clothes and have whatever I needed sewn on the spot. There seemed little point in lugging clothes along when they could be custom made so easily and inexpensively. I could choose material, order a skirt and matching shirt, and pick them up the following day—with a perfect fit—for less than four dollars. Fabulous!

Years after my return from Nepal, I read a sentence in one of Jane Goodall's biographies that inspired me to think about the clothes hanging in my closet. Along with other adventurers and explorers, Jane Goodall had become one of my childhood heroes, and I vividly remember watching programs about her on television at the age of nine or ten. Her life both captivated and inspired me in my quest for knowledge.

In one of her biographies, I was struck by her observation that most people of the Western world had enough clothes to outfit an African village for years. I'm not exactly sure what attracted me about this phrase, but it started me thinking. I reached for a piece of paper and began writing a list, checking off the various types of clothes that filled my closet. Enough clothes for hiking, enough for the gym, enough for skiing, enough for work, and enough for the occasional need to dress up, perhaps for the opening reception at an art gallery. Then, I thought about linens. Enough sheets, enough towels. As my list continued to grow, I realized I didn't need anything, nothing at all.

I thought I'd try an experiment. I would buy nothing for one year. No clothes, no sheets, no shoes, not even socks. It actually seemed like a fun game, as I never enjoyed shopping. My friends told me that I didn't shop. Rather, they said, I bought. I didn't know what this meant until they explained that a shopper goes to five or six stores, checks out the prices, and perhaps the quality, before making a purchase. Instead, a buyer goes to one store, and if she finds what she wants, she makes a purchase. The idea of going to several stores sounded both exhausting and like a waste of time, not to mention boring. I might see someone wearing a shirt I liked, or maybe a pair of shoes, ask her where she purchased them, go to that store, make the purchase, and shopping was completed.

That sentence by Jane Goodall inspired me to not buy anything for one year. My friends thought my idea crazy, and they couldn't understand why I would deprive myself of shopping. I told them that I didn't feel deprived. Rather, I was intrigued to know how it felt to buy nothing for one year. At the end of that first year, I experienced no sacrifice. In fact, since I felt no effect, I embarked on a second year of no shopping. Three years passed before I felt the need to purchase any clothing, linens, or shoes.

Years ago, I heard Jane Goodall speak at a local high school. I was working with teens, helping them with their academic studies. The mother of one of my students called a couple of hours before our appointment saying she wanted to cancel her child's session. My twenty-four hour cancellation policy encouraged students and families to be accountable and responsible for their appointments. I asked the mother why her daughter would not be able to attend the lesson. When she told me the high school was hosting a presentation by Jane Goodall, I said not to worry about the missed lesson. Her daughter would learn far more from Jane Goodall's talk than from spending time with me, reviewing her math assignments. And it gave me a chance to attend the presentation, to finally meet in person one of my childhood heroes.

I have often preferred the simplicity of few possessions, a continual struggle in our well-to-do, material-ridden culture. Wide-open spaces, whether in the landscape or in the room of a home, inspire me. I treasure emptiness, as from emptiness comes both ideas and imagination. If a vase remains continuously filled with flowers, no room beckons the creation of a beautiful bouquet. Thus I sometimes put an empty vase on a table, awaiting the arrival of something beautiful. And when I find myself in a store, as I walk down the aisles, I mentally repeat to myself, "All the things I do not need." This helps me stay focused on why I came into the store and makes the task less overwhelming.

∾

OUR GROUP PROCEEDED UP the trail—myself, Paul, Sidny, and Peyton, and our support team, which included one guide and five porters, of which one was the cook. At the last minute, a change of plans occurred. Our guide, Sergie, couldn't make the trip as his father had passed away. Instead, he asked his friend, Dende, to be our guide. Dende came from the Khumbu region, which would come in handy, as he knew both the terrain and the people of the small villages. The porters included Santa, Dawa, Serle, Krishna Budar, and Tenzing.

We kept to the foot path, rather than the road, and walked for about an hour from Kirantichap to the small village of Busti. We crossed our first suspension bridge of many, the bridge swinging precariously above a raging river swelled from the recent monsoons. Often these bridges lacked numerous footboards and could be challenging to cross, in addition to outright terrifying. And sometimes the bridges no longer existed, having been washed away by the monsoons, requiring long detours. Fortunately, the bridge before us had survived the rains, and Busti lay just across the Bhote Kosi River.

Although I walked slowly, I felt tired and sweated profusely from the long, uphill climb. Paul commented that I hiked at a good pace, taking it slow and adjusting to the altitude. He said Sidny and Peyton hiked too fast, and Dende confirmed this, noting we would not be able to walk so quickly when we reached Namche Bazaar at an elevation of 11,286 feet.

Finally, we stopped for a breakfast of bread, jam, and cheese, along with a hot meal of curried noodles and potatoes, followed by tea. I ate quickly, starving from the morning hike. As we continued hiking, I became aware that Nepal fit into a very different time and space than the place where I lived back home. The pace was certainly slower, and the rhythm of life slower. Distances were calculated and measured by how far you could walk in a day and what you could carry on your back. Even though weeks stood between the high mountains and me, I could feel their energy permeating the landscape.

Mountains of over 22,000 feet surrounded me, holding me within their magnificent hands, a tangible feeling I could almost taste.

In periods of difficulty, I often sought the company of nature for perspective and understanding. I had learned to appreciate the larger cycles of time that governed great mountain ranges. Knowing they would still be there tomorrow, in the same form, with their same majesty, offered me comfort from the constant wavering of life; the impermanence of all things. Although even the mountains would someday be gone, they provided me with a solid bedrock upon which to temporarily rest.

I continued walking slowly, and by the time we stopped for lunch, the anxiety I had felt in the morning had faded away. The last to arrive, I huffed and puffed up the steep hills. The porters cooked a lunch of rice with swiss chard, or perhaps spinach, the food tasting delicious, like the earlier breakfast. We brought along our own utensils, as spoons were seldom available. The Nepalis ate their food with their right hand. An important custom was to not touch food with one's left hand, as Nepalis used the left hand for cleaning after defecating, thus making it offensive to see it used for food. The left hand could be used for picking up a glass or holding something nonedible.

The local people stared at us as we walked along. An oddity, I felt their eyes upon us. As we walked through one village, the local market ended and the villagers broke down the produce stalls. I stopped for a moment to rest and eat a snack of nuts and raisins. But not yet comfortable with the stares, I quickly threw my rucksack over my shoulder and resumed walking down the trail.

We continued hiking toward the village of Yarsa. As the sun disappeared behind mountains and my legs trembled from the continual uphill climb, I became aware that I had lost the trail. Unfortunately, this occurrence would arise again in a more precarious situation farther up the trail. Once I realized my predicament, I waited for the porters, who walked far behind me, as exhaustion and the deepening darkness prevented me from continuing alone. I arrived at camp completely spent and hungry again.

The campsite stood high up on a hill and overlooked the steeply terraced, mountainous slopes sparsely dotted with houses. Glorious hiking weather accompanied us throughout the day, a huge, blue sky arching overhead, sprinkled with a sea of white, puffy clouds. But the humidity remained high, the excessive moisture from the recent rains hanging over the land. As I settled into camp, I took care as I discovered the entire area was filled with leeches, the first one firmly attached on my right thigh.

I didn't mind spiders, snakes, or most insects, but leeches made me squeamish. I didn't like things that attached themselves to my skin and fed off my body. They looked innocuous enough, resembling nothing more than a small twig. But within a short time, they swelled up into large, fat, black blobs as they fed off their victim. I carefully picked off the leech and kept watch during the evening for more intruders. It was an early night after another delicious meal of rice, dahl, and potatoes seasoned with curry, garlic, turmeric, and chili. The clear skies and numerous stars quickly disappeared as clouds moved in across the glorious night sky.

A pattern developed that continued for the next few months. I rose at about five in the morning, started on the trail by eight, stopped for a long lunch as the porters rounded up food and cooked the hot noonday meal, and then continued hiking, usually alone, until just before dark. The porters went ahead of us so they could begin cooking the noon meal, and again later in the day, so they could set up our camp before we arrived. This pattern, of me trailing at the end of the group, caused problems as we climbed to the higher elevations.

I awoke on the third day at five fifteen to a cool morning, and the pattern continued. With the fog heavy and the air wet, humidity hung in the air. One of the wonderful things about these early mornings was the rich tea and biscuits served to my tent. The Nepali people drank black tea with milk and lots of sugar, like the common spice teas of India. Because of their divine taste, I thought it wouldn't be too difficult to get up early at home if someone brought me tea and biscuits in bed. After tea, we packed and were on the trail by eight.

The trail climbed steeply up a mountain and I walked slowly. As the day unfolded, the fog dissipated, and the blue sky returned with the same large, white, puffy clouds filling the wide, open space overhead. I munched on nuts and raisins, but my hunger continued, as my routine did not include hiking without first eating breakfast. I needed food before noon.

We stopped for our first meal of the day just past the village of Chisapani. The porters prepared a main meal of rice with a cooked green vegetable somewhat like squash, bright green in color. After the meal, we continued with a long descent, followed by another long climb after two more river crossings. It seemed each day this pattern repeated. We began with a steep climb up a mountain, followed by a descent down the other side, then a major river crossing or two, followed by another steep climb up another mountain. I wondered if the schedule would ease up a bit. It would be lovely to arrive at camp before dark, but every day the hours of daylight shortened as the season deepened into fall.

At a quiet spot along the trail, I stopped and bathed in the river—though cold, wonderfully refreshing. I stopped to bathe while the sun still shone so I wouldn't get too cold as the light faded behind the mountain peaks. Thus, another pattern began. I often washed out an article or two of clothing and hung it on the back of my pack to dry. At the lower altitudes, it would dry by the time I arrived in camp, and at the higher altitudes, I gave up washing clothes.

We stopped at a teahouse at four in the afternoon and I took some photos of the small children that showed great curiosity in us. They crowded around us whenever we entered a new village. By the time I arrived at the teahouse, Paul, well-rested and ready to leave, uncharacteristically expressed impatience with the slow hiking pace of the porters. He complained the porters moved too slowly behind us. Although some of the porters may have begun hiking after us in the morning, most of them went ahead of us to set up camp, get organized, and start cooking. But sometimes, they temporarily lagged behind, especially if they met someone they knew in one of the villages. Paul saw little point in hiking on ahead as the porters carried our tents. I felt fine, free of anxiety, most likely too tired to exert any additional energy. I enjoyed that the porters lagged behind since it meant that I kept up, no longer the slowest hiker of the group. I preferred walking at a slower pace, enjoying the incredible scenery, stopping to take photos, and taking in the endlessly remarkable landscape.

Sidny and Payne, along with Paul, usually hiked ahead of me, often miles ahead. Sometimes I'd see Sidny and Payne before they headed out in the morning, but usually they left before me. This was a distinct change from hiking with friends at home, where I set the pace, usually taking the lead. In Nepal, although at the rear, I enjoyed the quiet of hiking alone.

Just before we reached the village of Those, two saintly looking men passed me on the trail, their faces beaming with light. They moved by me like two balls of light drifting past, leaving a feeling of peace permeating the air. The men did not appear to walk. Rather, they floated by, as though not part of the physical world, which firmly anchored me. Energy and light radiated from them. Their style of dress, quite different than anything I had seen so far, caught my attention. Their long, brown robes made of a coarse fabric, in addition to the absence of any belongings, suggested they were on a pilgrimage. I wondered what they did for shelter when night fell, or what they ate along the way. It seemed they did not have the same earthly needs as I.

Later in the afternoon, when I caught up with Paul, he asked me, "Did you see the wandering Shiva sadhus?" He explained that the first pilgrim carried a Shiva staff, a three-pronged walking staff with the Hindu image of Shiva carved at the top. I had failed to notice this as the extraordinariness of the two men captivated my full attention. I couldn't imagine coming across two such people on a hike in the Sierra mountains of home and felt grateful that I had witnessed such a unique experience.

Wandering sadhus represent an ancient Hindu tradition in India and throughout Asia. In Sanskrit, sadhu means holy man, sage, or ascetic. Sadhus renounce conventional life styles, choosing to live apart from or on the edges of society to focus on their own spiritual practice. They leave behind material attachments, often dress in saffron-colored clothing, and may retreat to caves, forests, and Hindu temples across India and Nepal. A sadhu seeks liberation, the fourth and final stage of life, through meditation and contemplation of Brahman, which represents the ultimate reality of the universe in the Hindu tradition.

Widely respected for their holiness, today four to five million sadhus wander across India. Many believe the austere practices of the sadhus help burn off their karma and that of the community at large. Thus, seen as benefiting society, sadhus traditionally receive support through the donations of local villagers. As the two Shiva sadhus floated past me, my thoughts quietly centered on peace, and I continued walking to the village of Those.

By the time I reached Those, darkness had fallen. In the last two days I had hiked nineteen miles, and my feet and legs ached. Barely conscious of them anymore, numbed beyond pain, I could feel the muscles in my calves tightening and my shoulders rebelling.

In Those, we camped in the open field of a school. We entered through a break in a stonewall, and the porters cooked our evening meal in the nearby school building. Just over the stone wall, a short path wound toward the river, which I could hear as I fell asleep, my body too exhausted to do anything other than collapse in my tent.

The following day, I awoke to my twenty-ninth birthday, September 28. One of the porters,

Serle, greeted me with tea and biscuits shortly after five in the morning, followed by a steaming bowl of porridge.

I savored these simple pleasures. One of the many aspects of backpacking I enjoyed was the distillation of activities to the present moment, my complete attention focused on putting one foot in front of the other or completing some mundane chore like preparing drinking water.

I packed up my belongings and hit the trail shortly after seven for an early start. Climbing up the path, though my feet and legs were completely exhausted as I took each step, there was no room to question the day. Just continue on as before, another cycle. Climb one steep mountain, descend the other side, cross a rickety suspension bridge over a raging river or two, and climb another steep mountain. Eat dinner, if not too exhausted, before collapsing into a deep sleep.

I followed along the river bank of the Jiri Khola River for one and a half hours to the town of Shivalaya, where I stopped for tea and brought out my relished supplies of bread, jam, and peanut butter. I savored these small treasures of food as though they were the rarest of goods, comforted by their familiarity.

The trail began to steeply climb away from the river valley, up and up and more up. My hiking slowed and my attention focused on putting one foot in front of the other, nothing more. My thoughts drifted to a simpler, easier "vacation." Perhaps on the way home I would stop in Hawaii, the type of vacation I rarely took and the usual, relaxing trip most people counted on every year or two. My mind began its chase, like a playful puppy, running from one place to another. Miles away from the steep climb before me, I basked in a cool, tropical breeze surrounded by the gentle roll of waves on a distant Hawaiian beach. I drifted from one daydream to another: colors of aquamarine, the touch of warm sand, and the feel of soft, gentle breezes, until at last, I returned to the present and continued hiking to the next village.

I approached the town of Buludanda, and the porters had already prepared the noon meal of cooked potatoes and vegetables. As I lunched, women threshed rice in a nearby clearing and men worked on a small house. After leaving the river, the trail climbed uphill for hours. By 2:45 p.m., I reached the small village of Deorali at the top of the next mountain. Although it was in the sun, the fog began to roll in, covering the mountain peaks, providing relief from the morning sun, my arms and face already weathered and dried from the crisp mountain air.

Our guide, Dende, decided that we would continue on to the village of Bhander, another hour down the trail. Well, maybe an hour for him, but two hours for me, as the downhill was even slower, my feet and knees aching with the long decent. As I approached Bhander, the landscape opened up to grazing hills and I heard the soft singing of chants as we entered the village. A wonderful welcome greeted me as I walked past the wall of carved stones, the mani stones, careful to keep them on my right.

Om Mani Padme Hum

Hail to the jewel in the lotus

NEPAL, A SMALL COUNTRY extending 500 miles east-west and 150 miles north-south, divides into three strips. The northernmost strip, the mountainous Himalayan country, includes eight of the ten highest mountains of the world. People who practice Tibetan Buddhism settled sparsely in the Himalayan region, and this was my destination, the Solu-Khumbu. The Terai, the southernmost and narrowest region of the three strips, extends north from the Indo-Gangetic plain of northern India, a hot and humid landscape. People who practice Hinduism settled here. In between the two outer strips lies an interface region of hills and valleys where the capital city of Kathmandu sits.

Because of the country's forbidding mountains to the north and deadly malaria endemics to the south, a major power never successfully invaded Nepal. Closed to foreigners and foreign influence until 1949, the country did not officially open its doors to tourists until a few years later, shortly followed by the dramatic influx of westerners—as well as the Chinese and Japanese, among others—to summit the world's highest peaks. Climbers scaled ten of the fourteen 8,000-meter peaks within eight years.

On May 28, 2008, the monarchy that had ruled since the Shah dynasty of 1768 collapsed. Nepal endured a decade-long civil war between the government forces and the Maoist fighters, the Communist Party of Nepal. The armed conflict lasted from 1996 until 2006, when a twelve-point agreement ended the conflict. Nepal follows a muti-party system, which saw Ram Baran Yadav elected as the country's first president in July 2008. Nepal ranks as one of the few countries in Asia to abolish the death penalty and the first country in Asia to rule in favor of same-sex marriage. With a population of 26.5 million in the 2011 census, Nepal holds the position of the forty-first most populous country in the world.

The Sherpa people arrived relatively recently to Nepal. Pangboche, their oldest village, and one of the highest, boasts of a history exceeding over three hundred years. The Sherpas speak a Tibetan dialect, dress like their Tibetan neighbors, and, at least in 1984, lived as traders and agro-pastoralists, farming their high fields of potatoes, wheat, barley, and buckwheat. They also herded yak and sheep in alpine pastures up to 17,000 feet.

Their region divides into three subregions: Solu, Pharak, and Khumbu. Solu, to the south, includes such villages as Junbesi and Phaphlu, with valleys reaching approximately 9,000 feet. Pharak stands between Solu and Khumbu along the steep banks of the Dudh Kosi River. Most Sherpa mountaineers hail from Khumbu, the highest of the three regions, ranging from 11,000 feet and up. Their villages include Namche Bazaar, Thami, Khumjung, Kunde, and Pangboche, as well as the beautiful Buddhist monastery of Tengboche. Among the Sherpas, the practice of Tibetan Buddhism pervades.

Throughout Nepal, the presence and symbols of Buddhism fascinated me. Rather than a religion, it seemed to be a way of life. Even the most humble dwelling held an altar inside with a photo of the Dalai Lama gracing the home. The many prayer flags, prayer wheels, and mani stone walls that adorned the villages and mountain passes delighted both my eyes and my spirit. They brought a feeling of lightness and contentment to me, and it became a welcome sight to see the colorful flags fluttering in the high mountain winds.

Even the smallest village had its beautifully painted water wheel sending out prayers across the land. Exquisitely painted, they ranged in height from less than a foot to five feet, six feet, or even higher. Built over a stream, water passed underneath, the wheel turned, and prayers were released into the air. Inscribed blessings decorated the outside of the prayer wheels, while scraps of papers with blessings printed on them filled the inside.

This wonderful tradition warmed me. Here was something that served absolutely no purpose, no function, other than sending out blessings across the land. Quite a different reason to build something than my Western training had taught me, in which function alone usually predominated.

Upon approaching or leaving a village, I often encountered mani walls and prayer wheels. Following the lead of my Sherpa guides, I learned to pass the mani walls and the prayer wheels on my right side and to spin the prayer wheels as I passed. According to Buddhist doctrine, it was important to pass the wall in the clockwise direction, the direction in which the earth and universe revolved. When an individual spins the prayer wheel, it is said that the effect is the same as reciting the mantra as many times as it is duplicated within the wheel.

The mani walls consist of intricately carved stone tablets, most of them inscribed with the saying "Om Mani Padme Hum," which loosely translates as "Hail to the jewel in the lotus." This mantra invokes the quality of compassion and it is said that within it are all the teachings of the Buddha. Most numerous in the high country of the Khumbu and intentionally placed along the roadsides and rivers, the stone tablets also formed mounds or cairns, especially on the top of mountain peaks and passes, representing an offering to the spirits of place.

The colorful prayer wheels accumulated wisdom and merit, also known as good karma, and purified negativities, or bad karma. Each wheel was beautifully and lovingly decorated with a mantra written in a clockwise direction to reflect the movement of the sun across the sky. Rolls of prayers and scripture resided inside the wheel, while devotees spun the wheels in a clockwise direction as they passed.

Over the months, I saw enormous prayer wheels, some taller than I and up to a meter wide. Filled with prayers written on paper and animal hides, they spun around as the wheel turned, releasing their prayers. There were also prayer flags throughout the landscape.

Brightly colored prayer flags lined the suspension bridges across Nepal's many rivers. Years later, I saw similar sights in Bhutan, a small Buddhist country nestled between China and India. After witnessing the transformation of Nepal over the last thirty years, Bhutan was making a valiant effort to retain its traditional culture and way of life in a growingly mechanized world dominated by Western values.

Traditionally, Tibetan Buddhists believe the prayer wheels and flags bring benefit to all, promoting peace, compassion, strength, and wisdom. They believe the prayers and mantras—blown by the wind, spread good will and compassion. I thought this a wonderful concept and never tired of seeing the flags blowing blissfully in the constant winds, their sole purpose to send prayers and goodwill over the village and countryside. I couldn't help but think perhaps it would be a helpful addition to our Western culture. It certainly couldn't hurt.

The flags, historically printed using wood blocks carved with mantras, came in sets of five. The colors represented the elements: yellow for earth, green for water, red for fire, white for air, and blue for space. Today, although commercially printed, they retain their beauty and meaning. In contrast to the prayer flags, carving both mani stones and walls requires significant collective effort and time. Similarly, prayer wheels demand devotion and time to prepare the prayers and decorate the wheels with beautiful colors and writings.

Many people recite the mantra thousands of times in a day as part of their daily prayer practice. Most Tibetans recite the Om Mani Padme Hum prayer, even though many of them do not know its meaning.

A wonderful story sweetly illustrates this: a devoted meditator, after years of concentrating on a particular mantra, attained enough insight to begin teaching. Though the student's humility was far from perfect, the teachers at the monastery were not worried.

A few years of successful teaching left the meditator with no thoughts about learning from anyone. But upon hearing about a famous hermit living nearby, the opportunity was too exciting to be missed. The hermit lived alone on an island at the middle of a lake, so the meditator hired a man with a boat to row him across to the island. The meditator was very respectful of the old hermit. As they shared some tea made with herbs, the meditator asked him about his spiritual practice.

The old man said he had no spiritual practice, except for a mantra, which he repeated over and over to himself.

The meditator cheerfully noticed as the hermit repeated the same mantra he used himself. But when the hermit spoke the mantra aloud, the meditator was horrified!

"What's wrong?" asked the hermit.

The meditator replied, "I don't know what to say. I'm afraid you've wasted your whole life! You are pronouncing the mantra incorrectly!"

"Oh, dear! That is terrible. How should I say it?" asked the hermit.

The meditator gave the correct pronunciation, and the old hermit was very grateful, asking to be left alone so he could get started right away.

On the way back across the lake, the meditator, now confirmed as an accomplished teacher, pondered the sad fate of the hermit. He thought, it's so fortunate that I came along. At least the hermit will have a little time to practice correctly before he dies. Just then, the meditator noticed the boatman looking quite shocked and turned to see the hermit standing respectfully on the water, next to the boat.

The hermit humbly said, "Excuse me, please. I hate to bother you, but I've forgotten the correct pronunciation again. Would you please repeat it for me?"

"You obviously don't need it," stammered the meditator. But the old hermit persisted in his polite request until the meditator relented and told him again the way he thought the mantra should be pronounced. The old hermit said the mantra very carefully, slowly, over and over, as he walked across the surface of the water back to the island.

My face still breaks into a large smile when I hear this wonderful story.

∾

IN 1984, STILL A sleepy country with little infrastructure, most of the population of Nepal lived in rural areas without road access. Walking was the only means of reaching most destinations since Nepal possessed the fewest miles of roads in proportion to area or population of any country in the world.

Nepal contained a population density of 110 people per square mile in 1984. By 2017, it soared to 202, an almost two-fold increase. Thus, ten Nepali people in 1984 equaled twenty people today. Not only had the sleepy country, open to tourists for little more than fifty years, entered the modern age, but also tourism had exploded.

In 1994, while traveling in Tanzania, Africa, I met an expedition leader from one of the major US trekking companies. He had led trips in Nepal for over ten years, and he now led this one trip up Mount Kilimanjaro in eastern Africa. He told me that in 1984, ten thousand trekkers hiked in Nepal, and by 1994, the number increased by twenty fold to 200,000. This gives an idea of how few people I saw on the Himalayan trek compared to just ten years later.

Television had been introduced to Nepal the year before my journey, in 1983, and the influence of Western culture penetrated quickly into the ancient traditions of the country. As I walked around the city of Kathmandu the days before our departure, televisions flashed in shop windows, along with posters of Michael Jackson and other well-known icons of the west. American culture stampeded through the country at an alarming rate.

With aid from India in the early 1950s, Nepal built its first paved road, connecting Kathmandu with Raxaul, on the Indian border. The terrain required costly building and maintenance, and landslides occurred frequently across the hilly areas during monsoon season. The rains compounded the problems, making the levels of several rivers and creeks difficult to predict. All of these factors contributed to periodic slowdowns in the movement of trucks and buses bringing essential supplies to the people. Nevertheless, as a result of road expansion, several private firms ran passenger buses and trucks to transport goods. From 1980 to 1990 alone, the number of passenger vehicles increased by more than one hundred percent. By mid-July 1989, approximately 2,900 kilometers of paved roads covered the country, forever changing the mountain landscape.

By 2007, although a study revealed that the country contained 10,142 kilometers of surfaced roads, 33 percent of the population lived at least a two-hour walk from a road. This presented a major challenge to economic growth, as well as difficulty for the local population in receiving education and health care.

Recently, the Nepali government announced a plan to build a one-hundred-kilometer paved road from Jiri, where I began walking, to Lukla, high in the Everest region. Tour organizers had long urged the government to build a road linking the Everest region to Kathmandu as an alternative to either the long trek or the unpredictable flight into the Khumba. Indeed, some trekkers wanted the new road built, as it would allow them to skip the multi-day walk up to Lukla. Perhaps by now, the road nears completion.

Trekkers and mountaineers that headed for Everest usually flew into Lukla's Tenzing-Hillary Airport, at an elevation of 9,380 feet. They began hiking from Lukla. Inclement weather often disrupted flights to Lukla, making trips to Everest both chaotic and expensive, as well as dangerous.

Arrival by plane revealed breathtaking and jaw-dropping scenery, some of the most spectacular in the world. As the plane descended, a tiny gray strip of tarmac appeared in the distance, almost completely camouflaged by surrounding greenery. This 65-by-1,500-foot patch of asphalt served as the runway. At its southern end a 2,000-foot drop plunged into a valley. At its northern end stood a stone wall and a hairpin turn.

Accidents abounded. Between October 2008 and October 2013, four small aircraft headed for Lukla crashed, killing thirty-three people. Although the airport closes in fierce winds and poor visibility, weather in the mountains changes so rapidly that a flight may already be airborne when conditions become dangerous.

Lukla Airport was built in 1964 by the Himalayan Trust created by Sir Edmund Hillary. The objective of the airport at that time was to ease the transportation of supplies to the Khumba region. Before construction of the airport, people took the Jiri trail to reach Everest Base Camp. Jiri to Surkhe alone encompassed a nine-day trek. The Jiri-Everest Base Camp route retraced the footsteps of Sir Edmund Hillary and Tenzing Norgay in their historic expedition to Everest, which climaxed with the first ascent of the peak on May 29, 1953.

∽

LIFE IN A RURAL Nepali family often means living under precarious conditions. In a typical mountain village, poor households rely on the produce grown from a small plot of land with no irrigation facilities, which is subject to erosion every year. Traditionally, a womn usually lives in her husband's house along with his parents and siblings. The family house is made of stone and provides only one or two shared rooms, with cooking occurring over an open stove in the main room.

Families with some wealth may own livestock such as cattle or chickens. Since very little can be set aside from year to year, most people cannot afford basic necessities. Such pleasures as a varied diet, clean water, fuel, medicines, decent clothing, and electricity may not be available. Often considered a luxury that detracts from the time the girls can spend working, educational opportunities remain sparse for females. Water, drawn from a local stream, must be carried to the fields and home. Dependence on firewood results in severe deforestation, the women walking hours to forage in the surrounding hills. Furthermore, health facilities remain limited. When a member of the family falls sick, he may be carried along treacherous mountain paths for hours to reach a health post. And often, the men in the household must leave the village in search of jobs to help support the family.

In the 1980s, life expectancy in Nepal remained in the high thirties to low forties. At that same time, life expectancy hovered in the seventies in the US. By comparison, today Nepal ranks 166th in the world with a life expectancy of 67 years, while the US ranks 42nd in the world at just under 80 years.

In 1984, Kathmandu boasted a reputation as a traveler's paradise. To the weary young backpackers that traveled across Asia for months or years at a time, Kathmandu offered the Western pleasures one craved, particularly in the food department. Brownies, bagels with cream cheese, lasagna, and just about everything else could be purchased in the narrow lanes of the Thamel district of Kathmandu. Travelers could also find the latest mountaineering gear in the numerous shops lining the rustic streets. Climbers from all over the world often left their supplies of jackets, boots, packs, and other equipment in Kathmandu, opting not to lug them home. If they had forgotten to pack a particular item, travelers could purchase the gear they needed.

I saw large, barrel-shaped, black plastic containers marked "rice" on the outside. Like the outdoor gear, the climbing expeditions left their surplus food behind instead of packing it out of the country. The barrels sat stacked in shops, silently awaiting the next expedition.

Just a block or two off the main road, the bustle of people and shops abruptly ended. Roads became dirt paths, narrow lanes coming alive at night with the local Nepali huddled around small fires as they cooked their evening meal. It was not until 2012 that I returned to Nepal. By the time I revisited Kathmandu, I could no longer recognize the city as it sprawled out to include several million people, no longer resembling the small town nestled in the valley I had known twenty-eight years earlier.

Days Opening From Above

Beauty is truth, truth beauty—that is all
ye know on earth, and all ye need to know.
—Keats

MY EYES FILLED WITH tears as I approached Bhandar. Coldness hung onto the village of Deorali, and I felt happy we did not stop there for my birthday. As I descended out of the fog into the open hills, I moved from dark to light, from forests to pastures, from green to gold. I passed the mani walls and monastery at the entrance to the village. As I walked with the wall on my right, I turned and entered onto a stone path with colorful prayer flags strung overhead.

A very special entrance welcomed me to the small enclave perched among such grandeur, nestled on a ledge with the mountains reaching high above and the valley stretching far below. As I passed the main teahouse, I noticed red geraniums gracing the upstairs window box, sunlight radiating off their bright petals.

Ahead of me, I saw Julian, the British doctor who had given me acupuncture treatments in Kathmandu, hiking along with his friend Sue. They remembered my birthday and presented me with a sweet gift, a strand of red yarn used by the local women as a colorful decoration in their hair. Touched by this simple act of kindness, tears welled up in my eyes. Light streamed through the clouds, breathtakingly beautiful as darkness arrived, the moon a whisper shining overhead. This being the first evening I was not completely exhausted, I set up camp and ate dinner. I felt peaceful and thought, what a grand place to spend the night of my birthday, as I lay down to sleep inside my precious tent.

The usual routine resumed the next day, with me rising at five. A surprise of apple pancakes greeted me for breakfast, and I left camp by eight. The next village, Sete, was seven and a half miles farther along the trail. As I headed down the path, the porter, Santa, gave me his walking stick, which I had admired yesterday. He soon found another and headed off down the trail carrying my olive-green canvas army duffel strapped across his back.

From Bhandar, the trail descended to the river and then followed along its bank. The sun's heat bore down through the clear morning skies as I walked at a slow, even pace, spending the first hour of the morning focused on each step. I stopped to bathe and continued on to Kenja, at an elevation of 5,360 feet, where the porters prepared lunch. While they cooked rice and potatoes, mixed with a few vegetables, I washed some clothes at the river's edge. By lunchtime, the usual large, puffy, white clouds had gathered. Afterward, the trail followed along the Likhu Khola River, a beautiful blue-green in color, still swollen from the rains.

From Kenja, the trail climbed steeply to the Lamjura Pass at 11,580 feet. I climbed and climbed and then climbed more. I walked through heavily forested areas and noted the large rhododendron trees. In Oregon, I had become familiar with the beauty of rhododendrons, their huge clusters of white, pink, and flaming-red blossoms screaming for attention, set off by striking dark foliage. Nothing shy about them. But the ones I knew from the northwestern United States rose perhaps six or eight feet, twelve feet at the most. At my side grew towering giants, trees fifty feet high or more, creating a beautiful forest along with the oak trees, also close friends from my distant home.

As I walked, I imagined the forests in the height of spring, bursting with color high overhead. As large trees with big, colorful flowers were not so common in the temperate climates, the sight of these majestic trees delightfully surprised and excited me.

At last, I reached the top of a ridge, not the actual summit, just the top of one of the many ridges that lay ahead. The porters, Santa and Krishna Budar, offered to carry my pack. I hesitated, as I was surely tempted. My pack weighed heavily across my back, but I felt I couldn't ask them to carry it. They carried enough. I would have felt embarrassed when the others found out, which I knew was ridiculously silly. Why did I care what they thought? I stopped and took a long rest. Santa told me it was one more hour to Sete, with a steep descent back down to 8,450 feet. I continued to focus on each step as I picked one foot up and placed it in front of the other. Exhausted and short of breath, I stopped often to rest.

In my mind, I could hear shouts of support along the trail cheering me on to the finish. When I finally arrived in Sete, I could hear my phantom support team shout, "Three cheers for Sylvia! You made it!"

The village of Sete emerged from the crest of a hill, resembling an eagle's nest atop a tree. With the fog rolling in and the sun's rays intermittently streaming through, Sete looked like it was about to take off, as a bird in flight. Far below lay an incredible view of the village of Kenja, with the Kenja Khola River Valley twisting its way through the mountains. The steep terrain cascaded down to the river with sculpted rice terraces and a few isolated houses dotting its flanks.

It amazed me that people not only lived at this altitude, but that they actually farmed the land. With no roads and no stores, only small trails connected one tiny village to another. Getting any supplies required a long journey, a treacherous descent to the river below, followed by a steep ascent up the far mountain. I tried to enter their consciousness, but our worlds remained too far apart to bridge the gap. Born locally, they tilled the soil and they died here. As I pondered this, I thought perhaps our lives were not really so different from one another. Weren't we all the same, doing our best as we went about the business of living?

As I walked along, my mind wandered into that difficult territory, wondering why I had the life I did? Why was I born in the United States, in California, and not in Rwanda or Bangladesh? I realized long ago that one either asked these questions or they didn't. For me, it was part of understanding what it meant to be human.

If in fact, I had chosen this time and place for birth, to be born again, as most of the world's population believed, how long had I taken to make the choice? A couple of days, a couple of years, or a few decades? Had I waited long for the right opportunity to present itself? One moment it seemed so clear, and the next the emptiness of the unknown overwhelmed me.

When my mother passed away, along with several other important people in my life within the span of a few short months, my thoughts kept revolving around death, and I considered what it meant to die. I read lots of books on the subject and I spoke with friends, but I found most people wanted to talk about death for only so long. For most of us, death remained an uncomfortable conversation and an uncomfortable thought process.

One day during this period, when the company of death surrounded me, I read a particular book on the space between dying and living. Although my Western training offered no definitive answers, I found the subject fascinating. Intrigued, I asked a friend what she thought happened after one died. It seemed a huge void existed in the conversation on this topic. My friend surprised me with her answer, saying that she had no interest in the subject. Unable to understand how one could not be interested in such a profound topic, I returned to the company of the many books that rose in piles about the house offering solace, insights, and perhaps understanding.

Sylvia at Gokyo Kala Patthar, about 18,000 feet, with Mt. Everest in background.

Mt. Everest

lvia and guide atop Everest Kala Patthar with Mt. Everest (left) and Mt. Lhotse (right) in background.

On the way to Gorak Shep, Everest Trek, about 17,000 feet.

Sherpas taking a break on the trail.

Local children walking on stone pathways in village of Junebesi.

108 water spouts at Temple of Muktinath, about 12,000 feet.

Near Jubing, Everest Trek.

View on Annapurna trek at harvest time.

Monkey Temple, Boudhanath Stupa, outside Kathmandu.

Gate at Junebesi, *original watercolor by Sylvia.*

Tents at Pheriche.

Yaks approaching Everest Base Camp.

Sherpa women on trail to Gorak Shep.

Thupten Chöling Monastery, near Junebesi.

Fellow trekkers enjoying a tea break on Annapurna Trek.

Sylvia entering a village via the prayer wheels.

Mountain Village, Junebesi, *original watercolor by Sylvia.*

Lake at Gokyo, *original watercolor by Sylvia.*

Young monk at Thupten Chöling Monastery, near Junebesi.

View from Gokyo Kala Patthar, about 18,000 feet.

❧

I NOTICED THE DELICATE, pink cosmos flowers blooming in the landscape around Sete. As the last rays of the sun washed the hillside in a golden light, I bathed and set up the tent. For a moment, the fog turned pink, then golden, and finally a whitish gray. Though the porters prepared a dinner of noodles, my body's exhaustion overruled again. Instead of eating, I drank tea and headed for the comfort of the tent, immediately sinking into a deep sleep.

The tent was set up "upstairs" on a platform above a teahouse, while the porters prepared food and slept downstairs. I slept until 5:40 a.m. and awoke to a clear blue sky with small wisps of clouds racing high above. With no fog, a warm day lay ahead.

Upon waking, I looked out from the tent to a steep ridge across the valley. I felt much better after my long sleep, and I noticed my calves and thighs were beginning to turn to steel. Although still rebelling, my body had begun to harden and strengthen as the days passed. I had walked forty-six miles since I left the bus six days ago near Kirantichap. My body told me that weeks or months had passed, certainly not days. Everything seemed new and different, my daily habits of home suspended as I adapted to my new environment in the Himalayas.

For breakfast, the porters prepared porridge and chapatis, a local flat bread, easy to make in the rustic conditions. I set out on the trail, another steep climb to the village of Goyun, at 10,550 feet. A forested landscape of rhododendron trees mixed with majestic oaks accompanied me, bringing a much-appreciated coolness to the air. With the cooler temperature, the porter, Santa, put on a beautiful, light-cream-colored shawl. He told me I could purchase a similar one in Kathmandu for 120 rupees. I touched the wonderfully soft wool, my fingers luxuriating in its comfort, making a mental note to purchase some for gifts to take home once I returned to Kathmandu.

At lunch yesterday, Santa had given me his walking stick, which he had so carefully smoothed out with his pocketknife. He took my walking stick back, the one he had given me earlier that morning. Decades before the use of hiking poles was common, I found the stick helpful as I continued climbing for hours toward Goyun. After a brief stop at the village, I continued climbing a bit more, winding through another rhododendron forest. Damp, gray fingers of fog came in and engulfed me, the coolness great for hiking.

Once again, for the thousandth time, the sheer beauty surrounding me overcame my senses. In addition to the grandeur of the landscape, I spotted a beautiful, silver-gray bird with a long tail and speck-led plumage sitting on a branch in the morning sun. Scattered along the trail, I noticed blue gentians, one of my favorite flowers in the alpine country of home, signaling the end of summer. Their pleated blossoms of striking blue violet hugged closely to the ground. Nearby, bright blue berries created a lovely carpet, and I followed the Sherpa's lead as he picked one of the berries and popped it in his mouth. It didn't taste unpleasant, but I didn't stop for more.

After a lunch stop, the trail continued its climb up the mountain. At the top of the Lamjura Pass at 11,580 feet, the sun peaked out from behind the clouds, and I took photos of the grand view and the small gentian flowers at my feet. Stones were piled high at the summit, marked with brightly colored prayer flags fluttering as the wind raced across the pass. Simultaneously, I felt the cooling breeze against my skin and the sun's warmth on my face. As I crested the top, I mentally etched the view that lay before me deep into my memory.

The trail began its steep descent, this time through luxuriant woods reminiscent of the Pacific Northwest. The maples turned brilliant gold, nestled like light bulbs within a thick forest of oaks, pines, and giant rhododendrons. As I descended, I often turned to look back and admire the beauty of the heavily wooded hillsides, dappled with sparks of luminescent yellows shining through the violet, blue, and green shades of the darkness of the pines.

The profusion of flowers continued with many gentians, white yarrow, and dark purple monkshood, familiar friends from the high country back home. As I hiked up the south side of the mountain, I looked across the river to the other side, the slope rising steeply, heavily forested with firs and maples. The trail wound around the mountain and dropped down into the village of Junbesi, covering another ten and a half miles.

Arriving just after five in the afternoon, I no longer cared that I walked the slowest of our group, or that the others hiked miles ahead of me. Comfortable with my pace, I established my own schedule, relishing the long periods of solitude with nothing but the mountain grandeur unfolding before me as I hiked higher and higher toward the sky.

I set up the tent in a cow pasture near a school, overlooking the valley below with a view of a river valley at my feet and high peaks towering above. A supreme luxury awaited, since we would stay in Junbesi for two nights. As I fell asleep, I noticed that the allergic reaction to the malaria medicine had almost run its course. Two weeks and three days had passed since the first outbreak. My skin continued peeling and clumps of hair continued falling out, but luckily thick hair graced my head.

As a child, my mother regularly thinned my hair. I would sit in the backyard, a chair set up on the grass. Mother would lift up the top part of my long, brown hair as she reached underneath, cutting away the strands below. As she continued, the grass became covered with dark clips of hair. Yet within half an hour of the completion of the haircut, I noticed the grass cleared of hair, green once again. Solving the mystery, I realized the sprigs of hair had been carefully picked up by the backyard birds, taken as material in the construction of their nests. This warm memory brought a smile to my face as I lay down in my tent, staked in a cow pasture just outside the mountain village, with the swollen river raging far below.

Junbesi, larger than the other towns I had hiked through, contained beautiful stone pathways winding throughout the village. Already hot by the time I awoke, Santa came to the tent, greeted me, and pointed to the distant view. He simply said, "Good view." I chuckled and agreed as I climbed out of the tent. A full view of Numbu Mountain rose in the far distance, its snow-covered peak soaring to 25,000 feet. Yes, a good view indeed. The porters prepared the usual breakfast of porridge and chapatis as I daydreamed about how to spend my free day. Should I take a day hike, wander around the village, get out my paints, or just take a nap?

On my treasured layover day, I decided to walk up to the local monastery with Paul and our guide, Dende. I hiked one hour up the hill to the monastery of Thupten Chöling. A lovely prayer wheel stood firmly below the monastery, sending out prayers and blessings as it turned effortlessly by the power of the stream flowing swiftly underneath. We entered the courtyard of the monastery and were privileged to meet the lama, Thulche Rinpoche. Previously, Dende had taken us to a small shop to buy the white, gauze-like scarves, katas, customarily given as a token of appreciation and respect upon meeting a lama. Though sometimes made of silk, these scarves were woven of a muslin fabric, a coarse, grayish-white scarf, that still hangs in my office today. Paul and I each wrapped the scarves around a five-rupee note and we presented them to the lama.

Dende translated for us as he and the lama spoke in Tibetan. Although I couldn't understand the conversation between Dende and the lama, I could tell a close bond existed between them. Feelings of serenity emanated from the lama and pervaded his dwelling. His eyes, timeless pools of quiet peace and joy, sparkled between elongated ears, resembling those of the statues of the Buddha. A gold piece of material hanging over the window bathed the room with a warm, golden light, while a few beautiful paintings and spiritual objects adorned the sparsely furnished room.

The lama asked where we were from, and he asked us our ages. We didn't speak much, but sat with him for about half an hour. As we left, he presented us with a red string to put around our necks and the white gauze scarf that we had presented to him, he now returned to us with his blessings.

We walked back to the courtyard and continued through to the gompa, a small temple of worship or religious learning. As monks busily recited scriptures, we walked around to the side. One of the monks approached us and invited us upstairs for tea. I watched as they prepared the tea in a beautiful traditional wooden flask. They served it with Khapche, a deep fried type of bread or pastry. As I sat drinking tea, the light in the room caught my attention. A rich, golden yellow in color, it fell over everything, and I drifted into a timeless place. I had no sense of being far from home or being in a strange place. All was calm, everything still, with a sense of familiarity emanating from the place. I stood there for a long time, until we quietly left through the courtyard, where large, flat wicker baskets of white cheese dried under the midday sun.

I spent the afternoon painting in Junbesi. Packed among my things, I had a tiny set of watercolors, a block of cold-pressed watercolor paper, and a small bamboo mat tightly rolled around two sable brushes, protecting them from breaking as I packed and repacked them on my travels. I completed two watercolors that day, one of the village against a background of the rising mountains, and the second of an archway across one of the village's many stone lanes.

As I painted, several children gathered around, curious about me and my paints. Upon entering a village, children followed in tow, bright eyed and eager to accompany us. They shouted "Namaste!" as their faces broke into wonderfully wide smiles. Namaste means "I bow to the divine in you," and accompanies the traditional greeting, done with the hands pressed together at the chest and a slight bow.

Painting relaxed me and helped me see things deeply and carefully. I felt as though I could get to know a place better by sketching or painting it. But I could not just arrive at a place and begin to paint. I needed to sit for a while and feel the place, allowing it to slowly seep into me, to become a part of me. Although I had carried my painting materials for days, I had not had a moment, let alone the energy, to pull them out earlier.

Over the course of the trek, I completed several small paintings. Years later, the painting titled "Gate at Junbesi" sold at an exhibit in San Francisco, along with many others. I withheld a couple of paintings from that show, not yet ready to part with them. Today, the ones not sold at that exhibition remain with me, and of those that sold, I can see them before me, clear as the day I painted them.

The following day I felt tired as I climbed another eleven miles to the village of Manidingma. With the exception of two foggy afternoons, the weather had remained glorious for days. I passed the quaint, little village of Ringmu, which appeared to have just one house, set on a hill surrounded by apple orchards, with snow-covered mountains rising in the distance.

I continued to climb a bit more and passed a monastery as the path began to descend down the other side of the mountain. The monastery was closed, so I continued on and followed the trail through a forested area to Manidingma.

Maples and firs made up the forest canopy, with ferns covering the floor. Numerous waterfalls poured down the steep slopes, creating walls of wet, lush vegetation alongside the cascading, vertical streams. With the brilliant fall colors, again my thoughts returned to Oregon, where I had collected many wonderful memories of the verdant forests and moist landscapes of the Pacific Northwest. For the entire morning, a range of snow-covered peaks came into view in the far distance. Beauty, beauty, and still more beauty surrounded me, and I was held within its far-reaching arms.

Yet, despite this grandeur, by afternoon I felt sick with an upset stomach. I suspected my body rebelled against too much hiking. Plain and simple. My body said enough and screamed at me in revolt. I rested a bit as the porters prepared a lunch of rice and vegetables, along with apple pancakes. I ate the pancakes, unable to stomach anything more, and continued into a long afternoon of more hiking until I arrived at camp at five thirty.

I set up my tent just outside a house in an area enclosed by a low stone wall. The sound of a stream gurgled nearby, and once again, a valley unfolded in front of me and I faced another mountain rising across the valley. Corn lay out on straw mats to dry just outside the house. A simple dinner of soup soothed me. But before comfortably settling in for the night, I discovered a tick at the top of my leg, so I crawled back out of my tent and Peyton helped remove it.

The ninth day of the trek, I slept until six, awakening to another day of clear skies. My best hiking day yet, I felt good and filled with a calm energy. This day represented the longest amount of time that I ever backpacked in the mountains. Thirteen years earlier, I had hiked for eight days in the California Sierras.

I spoke with Paul, saying that I would prefer a slower pace, as climbing one mountain, descending the back side, crossing a major river or two, and ascending another mountain each day was too much for me. Paul said that after Namche Bazaar, the pace would slow considerably. Once we reached the higher altitudes, we would be forced to slow down, whether we liked it or not. Inwardly, I hoped that I would be able to last that long.

I crossed the Dudh Kosi River to the village of Jubing, where I noticed a lone mailbox alongside a small hut. My thoughts drifted to home as Dende said it would take a letter ten days to reach Kathmandu, the same number it would take to hike to a place where I could speak with someone I knew. In other words, how many days it would take to reach a telephone.

Long before the days of the ubiquitous cell phone, it was possible to be completely out of range from others, to get unconnected. After understanding that it would take ten days for me to hike to a phone, I felt unsettled and alone, like a tiny speck unknown to the rest of the world. This realization surprised me. Since I had traveled extensively in developing countries, I did not expect to feel disoriented. Perhaps the remoteness along with the physical demands of the trip combined to create a feeling of uncertainty and vulnerability. Years later, still before the advent of the cell phone, I found myself in one of the three countries of the world that did not have AT&T service. Feeling the need to connect with someone I knew from home, I felt disappointed and isolated when I realized my calling card was of no use.

I continued hiking and reached Kharikhola by midafternoon, a wonderfully short day for which I gave thanks. As the town bustled with its market day, a game of volleyball began in a nearby clearing. I joined in the game with the Nepalis, comfortable now with these gentle mountain people, and I spent an enjoyable afternoon with them as the sun waned.

The tent was set up above a hotel, overlooking the village below. It rained most of the night, with the edge of the distant snow peaks visible just over the ridge.

Once again I fell asleep by eight.

The next day the rain ceased and I awoke to clear skies. Not surprisingly, a long uphill trek awaited me as I started out from camp at eight in the morning.

The landscape, breathtakingly beautiful as I hiked through thick bamboo forests, exploded in a rich, bright green color with dazzling, plump raindrops clinging to the leaves, dripping from the night's rain. It was lush like an equatorial rain forest with waterfalls cascading down the steep sides of the mountain as I descended. I continued up a valley with a view of a deep, narrow gorge and many more waterfalls visible across on the far side of the valley. An abundance of wildflowers still lined the trail, and ripe apples hung in a lone tree. I stopped to sample a bright red apple, delicious and crunchy, providing a welcomed break from the scarcity of available fresh fruit.

I hiked on another ten miles and arrived at the village of Surya in the late afternoon. I set the tent up behind a guesthouse and crawled into my bag for another early night.

The days passed with little sense of time. I awoke with the sun and I went to bed when darkness arrived. The days of the week carried no significance for me. One day flowed into the next, distinguished only by where we camped. The landscape changed, the clouds passed overhead, the sun and moon moved across the sky, and I kept putting one foot in front of the other as I hiked across the Himalayas, or more accurately up and down among the continuous range of mountains before me.

I awoke to a damp and foggy morning with little visibility—an easier day, with us hiking only nine miles or so to the village of Phakding. The morning fog cleared from town early, but it clung like a tight, gray wool cap to the mountaintops. The sun and fog played chase with each other as I hiked farther up the mountain.

I spent the day focused on my breathing. Paul had told us that it would be very helpful for our acclimatization to the higher altitudes, and would increase stamina. As I hiked, I practiced one full breath for every step. By walking slowly into the high country, my goal was to gradually increase the production of red blood cells and thus the amount of hemogloblin, the oxygen-carrying component of human blood: the same strategy athletes employ by choosing to train at high altitudes. Researchers have recently discovered that rather than elevated levels of hemoglobin, Tibetans have undergone unique genetic adaptations that have enabled them to thrive in a reduced oxygen environment. Most Tibetans are thus protected from chronic mountain sickness.

I also practiced double breaths on the uphills: two breaths in and one breath out. This filled me with energy as I climbed toward Phadking; the hours passed smoothly, us arriving in the early afternoon.

We camped in a pasture above a river winding its way through a narrow canyon below, sleeping to the sound of rushing water. Just across the river, the rock slope climbed steeply into the clouds. The fog nestled in close that night, with the moon rising briefly before it disappeared behind the gathering clouds.

The porters prepared a wonderful dinner of tomato soup. I enjoyed the soothing meal after miles of hiking, but my exhaustion prevented me from eating the accompanying rice and potato dishes. After dinner, the porters pulled out a flute and a harmonica. They sang and danced as we watched, sitting close by. But I couldn't stay up for long and retreated to my tent for another early night, exhausted by seven thirty in the evening.

The next morning as I peeked out of the tent, the first light rays greeted me as they quickly reached the snow-peaked mountains, surely the beginning of a great day. The usual routine continued, hiking by eight. With beautiful scenery alongside, I hiked up the Dudh Kosi River Canyon, plunging to the deep river gorge below. Swollen with the recent rains, the river moved swiftly, its waters muddied to a rich chocolate brown from the immense amount of soil and minerals it carried down the valley. I passed several waterfalls and crossed several more suspension bridges, each one seeming more treacherous than the last, never quite allowing me to get comfortable with them.

A view opened up to Thamserku Mountain, rising to 21,729 feet, with a clear sight of where the trees ended and the uninterrupted snow began. The landscape of the river canyon changed dramatically, with lots of rocks, perhaps granite, and steep cliffs rising on both sides. I thought of the California Sierras with their magnificent, large boulders strung across the sides of fierce canyons. The delicate leaves of the mountain ash and the majestic stature of the mountain hemlock also carried me back to the forests of California. As I passed these familiar trees, I also noted Himalayan white pine and the lovely blue pine, combining to form a thick forest.

While I continued hiking toward Namche Bazaar, the fog rolled in and the top of the river canyon disappeared into the white clouds, hidden like a treasure beneath the sand. The temperature quickly dropped and the wind ripped through the canyon. I climbed and climbed, farther up the steep slopes, constantly aware of the magnificent beauty surrounding me; the golden leaves of fall sprinkled in among the dark foliage of the evergreens and the forests held in the cup of the towering mountains.

By midafternoon, as I rounded the last corner and the town of Namche Bazaar came into view,

I noticed two yellow roses clinging to a small bush. With most of them long since transformed into rose hip fruits, I smiled as I thought how wonderful to see roses blooming at 11,000 feet. The gentians and monkshood flowers also stood out as I approached the town.

I walked by many gardens filled with vegetables and flowers, including colorful dahlias and pink cosmos, finding it truly remarkable that any gardens thrived at this altitude. I had first noticed cosmos in Mexico, years earlier when I studied fabric designing and brushed up on my Spanish before traveling farther south into Central America. Cosmos seemed so simple and cheerful, clear pink flowers filled with yellow stamen, growing along the driest and most forgotten stretches of dirt.

Above 11,000 feet

*The last bird flew away and then there
was just me and the mountain.*

F ROM NOW ON, I would be hiking in the high
country, at Namche Bazaar or above. Paul told
us about the possibility of altitude sickness, what
precautions to take to avoid it, and what to do if it
began. We planned each day carefully to do as much
as possible to avoid this dreaded sickness

Altitude sickness generally occurs at altitudes
of 8,000 feet and above, brought on by climbing to
higher and higher altitudes too quickly. People not
accustomed to these heights remain most vulnerable.
Symptoms, including headache and insomnia, can
develop into more serious difficulties. I followed the
prevention practices, and most fortunately, did not
experience altitude sickness.

Impossible to predict, age, sex, and general health do not affect risk. Altitude sickness occurs in 25 percent of travelers over 8,000 feet in Colorado, 50 percent of travelers in the Himalayas, and 85 percent of those in the Mount Everest region. When ascending rapidly and climbing more than 1,600 feet per day, the risk increases. Once any of the symptoms begin, one must descend to a lower elevation immediately. An important rule of thumb is to never hike toward a higher altitude, to sleep if experiencing symptoms, and to descend if they get worse while resting.

Two of the riskier ways to climb mountains is flying to a high altitude and beginning to walk from there, and walking to higher and higher altitudes too quickly. Thus we began hiking at the end of the road, choosing not to fly into Lukla, an airstrip located one to two days south of Namche Bazaar. We followed a cautious approach.

The body typically needs three to five days at altitudes above 8,000 feet to acclimate to the environment before traveling higher. Because the body doesn't have enough time to adapt to the lower air pressure and the lower oxygen level at high altitudes, it responds by increasing the breathing rate. In turn, this boosts the blood oxygen, but not to normal levels, and the body must adjust to operating with less oxygen than usual.

It is best when hiking above 10,000 feet to increase altitude by no more than 1,000 feet a day, and to build a rest day into the schedule for every 3,000 feet gained. Thus, our policy of "climb high and sleep low." Climbing more than 1,000 feet in a day necessitated returning to a lower altitude for sleeping.

∾

As I approached Namche Bazaar, orchards of apple, peach, and apricot trees graced the fields. Namche, as it was called for short, was a wash of brown and earth tones, with few native trees. Like two great arms, the mountain slopes encircled the houses as they terraced up the hillside. While the fog settled in, a lovely quality of peace enveloped the town and its people, the Sherpas. I set up the tent in a large dirt area behind a three-story house, which the porters used for cooking our evening meal.

Energized by the crisp mountain air, I headed off to explore the town and found a shop that sold cinnamon rolls. Smelling something divine, I discovered chocolate cake baking in the oven. Drifting to heaven, I bit into a large, warm cinnamon roll, vowing to return the next day for chocolate cake. Nearby, Tibetan women sold their wares in the numerous shops. I purchased a necklace like those worn by Sherpa women. Their necks bore heavy necklaces, weighted down with large pieces of turquoise, amber, and other gems passed along through the generations. Though I had seen quite a few spectacular ones, I bought a simple necklace made for tourists. Since the necklace cost only the equivalent of three dollars, I didn't bargain with the young woman, finding it difficult to squabble with those who have so little. How could I bargain over three dollars? As I gave the woman the money, she noticed a gold necklace with a stylized lotus hanging at the center encircling my neck. She expressed an interest in buying it, but I declined her offer.

In 1984, glass windows were a rare sight in Namche or any of the high mountain villages. Glass had to be carried in on foot for days or weeks from factories below. Instead, thick, green, wooden shutters covered the windows.

From Namche, the mountains kept popping up everywhere, like an endless sea extending to the horizon. I noticed the difference from the California Sierra Nevadas, a north–south mountain range extending for close to 2,000 miles from southern California north to the Canadian Border. They changed names a few times, the Cascades in Oregon, the North Cascades in Washington, but northward they marched. Despite their long distance and narrow width, they formed a central spine, one side gradually falling to the forested slopes of the west and the other steeply dropping to the high desert of the east. It was possible to stand on a peak of the spine and look out in both directions, east and west. This was not so in the Himalayas, where the mountains just went on and on, seeming to never end, as the vast ocean of peaks reached into the far distance.

My small notebook filled with sketches of the many beautiful birds I saw while I hiked through the forests. The white-throated dipper, as it hopped from rock to rock in the rushing river. It seemed to be pecking at the rocks, looking for small bits of food. And the white-capped river chat, with its brilliant, reddish, rust-colored breast and crown, and a similar color mixed in the tail. The rest of the bird was the color of charcoal. As I stepped across the mountain landscape, I saw several darting along the river from rock to rock. The bird, with a brilliant yellow patch on its wings, may have been an oriole, or perhaps a Tickell's leaf warbler.

In addition to painting, I enjoyed sketching the birds, flowers, and landscapes I came across as I hiked. I did a quick sketch showing the town of Namche, held within the slopes of the surrounding mountains. The town sat in a wide semicircle that opened out to the valley below, with high mountains framing the town on three sides. Namche, positioned so the houses faced east, caught the morning sun as it rose over the peaks. It was an exquisite and functional design; my years of training in the architectural fields could not have resulted in a more practical or beautiful layout. As I entered the high alpine country, trees no longer reaching the high altitude, muted tones of brown, tan, and gray washed across the barren land.

The thirteenth day provided a welcome rest day in Namche. With the skies perfectly clear, the sun struck the mountain peaks early. I awoke to frost on the tent. After a relaxing morning, I hiked to the village of Khunde at 12,667 feet, practicing the "hike high, sleep low" routine in preparation for the higher altitudes that lay ahead.

As I climbed, more and more mountain peaks became visible. The crest revealed the entire range, including Mount Everest (29,029), Lhotse (27,940), Lhotse Shar (27,503), Ama Dablam (22,349), Kangtega (22,251), and Thamserku (21,729) in the foreground. Although Everest rises over 6,000 feet higher than Ama Dablam, at first it is hard to notice. Because of the angle and perspective, it sits in the background and appears lower than its neighbors. Not until I reached the huts of Gokyo weeks later did I experience the full stature of Everest.

A breathtaking sight to behold, the view of Khunde opened up before me with even more earth tones than Namche. A series of stone walls crisscrossed the land, dividing it into individual plots for farming. Potatoes, potatoes, and more potatoes—one of the few crops that could survive at these heights. The terrain resembled a high desert with no trees in sight, and I passed many familiar plants as I hiked: crimson-red barberry bushes turned a deep hue with the shortening days, and lovely blue gentian flowers carpeted the dry plain. Small juniper trees dominated the landscape along with the barberry. With a clear view of Ama Dablam, Khunde lay ready to greet me.

I visited the medical clinic in Khunde, and also the home of a local artist who made stylized paintings of the village and surrounding mountains. I learned she and her husband had been friends of Sir Edmund Hillary back in his days of Himalayan explorations. The couple had traveled to New Zealand to visit Edmund, their modest house now filled with interesting photographs of their time together. I continued hiking to the Everest View Hotel only to find that it no longer operated, a lone abandoned building among the deserted landscape.

As I circled back toward Namche, the Himalayan birch trees radiated brilliance. Like lightbulbs their yellow leaves shone against the clear, blue mountain sky. Peace washed over me and I felt close to the heavens above as I hiked down the valley, almost too beautiful to behold.

Just outside the village of Khunde, I stopped at a small teahouse. Dende knew the woman who owned the shop. Upon our arrival in Namche, we had entered the home territory of Dende, the Kumba region, and he knew many of the locals in the small villages scattered across the mountains. This provided us with a great advantage in obtaining food from the scarcely available supplies. As I headed down the mountain to Namche in the late afternoon, fingers of thick fog settled snugly against the village, encircling it within their grasp.

From his numerous visits to the Khumba, Dende knew the local family of Sherpas who lived next to our camp in Namche. I enjoyed a beautiful evening with the mother and father, their two boys, and two girls. The daughter prepared the evening meal of mashed potatoes as we sat and listened to the horns from the nearby gompa. It sounded a bit like bagpipes, or perhaps a foghorn: a low, eerie sound every evening and morning as the monks played their instruments in the nearby courtyard.

The Solu-Khumbu region extends south and west from Mount Everest. Populated by Sherpas, the ethnic group became famous for their exploits on mountaineering expeditions. In 1984, less than 10,000 people visited the Khumbu each year. Ten years later, by 1994, the number had mushroomed to 200,000, and by 1999, almost 500,000 visited Nepal. For every person I saw in 1984, by 1994, twenty people stood in their place. I wonder how many hike on these mountain trails today? Perhaps fifty, one hundred, or maybe more—clearly, it is a different place and experience than in 1984. And all this for a country closed to the world until the mid-twentieth century.

As broadly known, Mount Everest, the highest mountain in the world, reaches a height of 29,029 feet. First measured by Indian mathematician Radhanath Sikdar, Everest was identified as the highest mountain in the world in 1852. The name Mount Everest comes from the British General and surveyor at that time, Andrew Scott Waugh, who named the mountain after Sir George Everest in 1865.

The Nepalese government gave Mount Everest a Nepalese name, Sagarmatha, in 1960. Most Nepali people refer to the mountain as Sagarmatha, meaning "Forehead in the Sky." Speakers of Tibetan languages, including the Sherpa people of northern Nepal, refer to the mountain as Chomolungma, Tibetan for "Mother of the World."

Sagarmatha, or Everest, straddles the border between Nepal and Tibet. The first recorded efforts to reach Everest's summit were made by British mountaineers. With Nepal not allowing foreigners into the country, the British attempted access via the north ridge route from the Tibetan side. After the first reconnaissance expedition by the British in 1921 reached 22,970 feet on the North Col, the 1922 expedition pushed the North ridge route up to 27,300 feet, marking the first time a person climbed above 26,247 feet. Tragedy struck on the descent from the North Col when seven porters were killed in an avalanche.

Two standard routes exist to climb the mountain. The first, the southeast ridge, climbs from Nepal. New Zealander Sir Edmund Hillary and Sherpa Tenzing Norgay took this route on the first ascent in 1953. Beginning with the Khumbu icefall at the base of Everest, one climbs up the western side to the South Col, continuing on to the southeast ridge.

The second route, the north ridge, climbs from Tibet via China. The famous 1924 expedition by the two British mountaineers, George Mallory and Andrew Irvine, resulted in the greatest mystery on Everest. They made a final summit attempt on June 8, 1924, but they never returned, sparking debate as to whether they were the first to reach the top.

They had been spotted high on the mountain that day, about eight hundred vertical feet from the summit, but disappeared in the clouds, never to be seen again, until Mallory's body was found seventy-five years later, in 1999, at 26,755 feet on the North face. The debate as to whether Mallory and Irvine reached the summit remains one of the most fiercely debated topics of mountaineering. Without recovering the camera that Irvine carried on the expedition, it may be impossible to ever prove if the two were the first to summit.

∾

AFTER THE CHINESE OCCUPIED Tibet in 1959, many Tibetans fled to the mountains of India and Nepal, settling in refugee camps. The northern border of Nepal was closed for years, but by 1984, restrictions had relaxed and trade could resume, though not as extensively as before. As I hiked across the mountains, I saw a country largely untouched by the ways and ideas of the West, with the growing exception of Kathmandu. On subsequent travels to Bhutan years later, I saw how that country had attempted to chart a different course after witnessing the Westernization of its neighbor, Nepal, over the previous thirty years.

In 1984, although not mandatory to hire a porter, it seemed right, as it supported the local people and cost so little, perhaps a dollar a day. We paid a bit more, three to five dollars a day, for our guide. Carrying a pack at sixteen thousand feet was not like a stroll in the woods, and the Sherpas provided a valuable service.

Nepal began its career as a trekker's paradise in 1949, when a British adventurer, Bill Tilman, secured permission from the King of Nepal to explore the high valleys of the Himalayan kingdom. Spectacular mountain scenery, picturesque villages, friendly people, and diverse culture, together with a network of superb hiking trails, made Nepal irresistible, and people kept coming back year after year.

After Nepal opened its frontiers to the outside world, mountaineers summited ten of the fourteen 26,000-feet peaks within eight years. Annapurna (26,545 feet) was the first to be climbed in 1950, by Maurice Herzog, who led a French expedition. Everest (29,028 feet) followed in 1953, and then Nanga Parbat (26,660 feet). The number of expeditions arriving from many different countries multiplied, and by 1964, all the Himalayan giants had been climbed, including Shishapangma (26,335 feet), scaled by the Chinese in 1964. Upon summiting Everest in 1953, Sir Edmund Hillary and

Tenzing Norgay made history as the first to reach the top of the legendary mountain.

Trekking in Nepal began as a sport after the many climbing expeditions. The sport took off with the first expeditions to the base of Everest, an American-led expedition in 1950 and a British one in 1951. Colonel Jimmy Roberts was the first person to realize that trekking would appeal to tourists. As a former Gurkha Officer and Military Attaché at the British Embassy in Kathmandu, he spent years walking the hills of Nepal. He accompanied Tilman on his first trek, and in 1964, he founded Mountain Travel, the first of Nepal's trekking companies and the inspiration for the adventure travel industry soon to follow.

Roberts' idea, revolutionary for the time, was to provide tents, together with Sherpas, to guide and cook for the trekkers. This made Nepal and the Himalayas available to a wide community, creating an immediate success. Roberts' Mountain Travel Trekking Agency, the first trekking agency registered in Nepal in 1964, remained the only one for the next four years. His first clients came to hike the Everest Trek in the early spring of 1965.

Dawa Norbu and Mike Cheney joined Roberts to handle the work at Mountain Travel. Early foreign partners included Leo LeBon, Allen Steck and Barry

Bishop from the USA, and the Australian Warwick Deacock of AusVenture. They regularly sent clients from their respective countries to trek in Nepal. Over the years, Mountain Travel prospered and became an inspiration for other Nepalese tourism entrepreneurs starting their own trekking and adventure companies.

Today, more trekkers than climbers hike in Nepal, because trekking is physically less taxing and provides other experiences apart from mountain climbing. Sir Edmund Hillary correctly stated Nepal provided one of the world's great trekking paradises. As I hiked along the mountain trails, it felt wonderful to have a sense of those who had come this way before me.

∾

THE NEXT DAY WAS a layover in Namche, and I slept until six thirty. I awoke to blue skies with the mountains shining clear and bright overhead. I walked to the bakery, purchased four cinnamon rolls, and asked Dawa to put a candle in one of them, as it was Peyton's birthday. We had a leisurely breakfast sitting in the sun, not departing until nine thirty.

We climbed out of the bowl in which Namche sat and headed toward the local museum. As it was closed, Dende encouraged some locals to open the doors, and we viewed an informative exhibit on the local plants, animals, and surrounding mountains that wrapped around us.

∾

MY LOVE AND APPRECIATION of the natural world began early in my life. I have many wonderful childhood memories of experiences with nature as a place of beauty, quiet, and solitude. Endless hours spent in the backyard digging in the dirt, making mud cakes, and wandering alongside the local creek nurtured my imagination.

As I waited for the bus to take me to nursery school, my sister and I would sit in the driveway making delicate flower chains, the sticky stem of a single flower of the pale blue plumbago stuck into the center of the next, linking them together to form a lovely necklace. Absorbed in the beauty and task before me, all sense of time disappeared. Unconscious of its passing, I surely would have missed the school bus if I had not been waiting right at the curb.

Across the street from my childhood home, a small creek wound its way behind the houses. I caught pollywogs and picked bunches of wild watercress for mother, as she loved the tangy, slightly bitter taste of the leaves. Grammar school nurtured a hobby of collecting wildflowers that continued for decades. Identified and carefully pressed flat between thick sheets of absorbent blotting paper, I noted the locations where I found them.

My sister and I would spend countless hours making beautiful bookmarks, pieces of white card stock with brightly colored flowers glued on them, sealed with plastic—somewhat like current day laminating. Over the years, the bookmarks grew in sophistication with sheets of elegant rice paper used as the backing, the flowers pressed in the middle, and the bookmarks edged with narrow strips of colorful satin ribbon along the sides.

I was fortunate to have two great teachers who helped cultivate my love of plants. The first, my sixth-grade teacher, Mr. Santel, introduced me to collecting plants and wildflowers for an extensive science report we kept the entire year. From him, I learned the importance of recording notes on the location and habitat where I found the plant as I prepared a sample on a sheet of thick, white botany paper. The second teacher, Mr. Farnham, taught my high school biology class. Animal cages and large glass containers of various sizes filled the classroom from floor to ceiling, covering all available space. They housed an impressive collection of live snakes, reptiles, turtles, mice, rats, and many other animals.

My love of plants, especially wildflowers, continued in my backpacking years as I carried one or two small, handmade plant presses with me while I hiked in the mountains. Upon returning home, I would transfer the collected flowers to a larger press. I loved learning the names of the plants and flowers, and they soon became my constant friends and mountain companions. Earlier, during college, I spent a summer studying at an environmental research station in Eastern Oregon, and I was offered a position teaching mountain botany.

∾

As I CONTINUED HIKING out of the Namche bowl, the trail traversed, climbing slowly around the mountain, every step bringing me closer to the peaks. It was autumn, the landscape bathed in a golden, yellow light. A low bush, *Euphorbia himalayensis*, covered the ground with a bright red-orange color along with cotoneaster, which created a groundcover full of pinkish-red berries. And the rose hips offered up a striking orange bronze color as a deep accent.

I hiked through a rhododendron forest, followed by a birch forest. The bark of the Himalayan birch, like fine translucent paper, exfoliated in sheets of crimson and orange. A strip of the papery golden bark still lays pressed between the sheets of my journal from so many years ago. Thousands of blue gentians continued to carpet the land, along with the precious edelweiss flowers.

The porter, Santa, stopped along the trail and pulled out several gentians from the ground, roots and all. He pulled the roots off each plant and the dirt fell away as he rubbed the bulbs in the palms of his hand. Once cleaned, he popped them into his mouth and explained that gentian bulbs brought relief to his cough.

The wealth of knowledge local people possess of their surroundings continually impresses me. Because it may be a matter of life and death, they learn at an early age which plants can help them and which to avoid, sacred valuable knowledge that would greatly benefit all of us, even us city-bound dwellers, whose lives revolve around the world of artificial drugs, most derived from the plant world. Sometimes I think when the world enters into another dark period in which our dependence on ready-made food and medicine is challenged, the people of traditional cultures will know how to survive.

∞

THE DARK SHADES OF the evergreens and juniper created a striking contrast to the brilliant fall colors. The forest burst with life and sang with color. As I left the rhododendron and birch forests, a small teashop came into view. Two Tibetan men stood in front of the shop with jewelry set out for sale on an old cloth lying at their feet. As I walked by, a silver bracelet with two small turquoise stones and one coral stone caught my eye. While I gathered some money together to purchase it, Dende greeted the two men, who were friends of his.

I continued hiking to Trashinga, where the porters prepared a lunch of pancakes and vegetables. After lunch, I descended down to the river and crossed the Dudh Kosi once again. Shortly after crossing the river, I came across six beautiful prayer wheels, positioned over a stream so that as the water flowed by, the water turned them, sending prayers out across the land, bringing blessings to all. Passing the village of Pungo Tenga, the trail began to climb steeply toward Thangboche, my destination for the night. As I climbed, the fog began to lift and I watched, mesmerized as the incredible view of Mount Mantegna came into view.

The entrance to Thyangboche, marked by an archway, created a wonderful sense of welcome to the town. After passing the gateway and walking a short distance around the gompa, I saw an amazing view open before me. A clearing in the foreground led up to the monastery, which terraced up the hillside. Beyond, the mountains glistened in the late afternoon sun. Straight ahead, Mount Everest reached high in the sky, with Lhotse and Lhotse Shar to the right and Island Peak behind. To the left was Lhotsthan. The view captivated me and held me within its spell for minutes before I could continue.

Fog danced in and out among the peaks, playing a game of hide and seek. That evening, the night sky was bright before the large moon rose over the mountains. The next day would be the full moon. I walked in the moonlight before dinner, enjoying the magnificence of this place, as the mountains disappeared behind a curtain of fog and the landscape was enveloped in peace.

Following, I had a rest day in Thyangboche. Hard to believe, but now I stood at an elevation of 12,660 feet.

I positioned the tent so the door opened out to a view of Lhotse, Lhotse Shar, and the ridge, with Everest rising up behind them. From moment to moment, the scene in front of me changed. The fog came in, the mountains disappeared; the clouds parted, and the sun burst through. The clouds closed in again, and so the cycle repeated itself, a beautiful reminder of the impermanence of life.

In the morning, I visited the monastery. Although beautiful inside, it did not feel as special as the one outside Junbesi. In the afternoon, I found a hot shower tucked into a tiny wooden hut in a field. It was lit by candlelight, and I floated to heaven as I let the water pour over me. The feeling of the hot water on my skin felt like such a luxury, and I melted into its warmth and softness. The fog created a quiet mood for the rest of the day, and I basked in the timelessness of the place.

Though my fifteenth day of trekking, it could have been one day, one month, or even years. Somewhere outside, a calendar kept track of the days, but the sense of time held no meaning for me, just one more day of putting one foot in front of the other and taking in the glorious views surrounding me. For now, that was all I needed to do.

The next morning, I awoke to an ill omen. One of our porters, Hasta Bahadur, had left. I couldn't find out the details other than Hasta Bahadur wouldn't sleep with the rest of the porters. He had slept up the hill, toward the monastery, and was gone by sunrise. I also awoke with a headache, which continued for most of the morning.

I began hiking toward Pheriche, a small outpost nestled in the barren gray landscape. Although only six miles up the trail, I walked at a slower pace. On the way, I stopped at Pangboche to see another monastery.

Though formidable at three hundred years old—the oldest monastery in Nepal—I was not impressed with the display of Yeti relics, including an old skull and bones of a withered hand.

As I continued hiking to Warsho, my pace slowed even more, moving like molasses across the dry landscape. The fog settled thickly over the land and the temperature plummeted. I hiked in two turtlenecks and the trusty, twenty-five-dollar, royal blue REI wind and rain jacket. The clouds parted for a moment to reveal a glimpse of Lhotse, and then they closed tightly again, taking the mountains with them. I reached Pheriche at four thirty in the afternoon, the temperatures hovering at forty to forty-five degrees with a strong headwind blowing up the canyon. I quietly set up the tent and prepared for a long, cold night. I now stood at 14,340 feet.

The days began later, with me rising at six thirty or so, instead of five. A rest day in Pheriche pleased me, as I felt lazy and somewhat disoriented. I spent the day watching the fog roll in and out, and the sun playing a continual game of hide and seek. I felt lonely, so far away from everything I was accustomed to. I yearned for familiarity, so I followed a routine that I knew. I bathed, I washed, and I walked. Lunch included a welcome treat of hot soup, potatoes, and an omelette, followed by more hours watching the fog close in around me.

I got out my painting materials and found a place to paint out of the wind. Painting was a new experience at this altitude and in this cold weather. As I worked with my small set of watercolors, I applied the brush to the paper. The water became thicker and thicker until I realized it was turning to ice on the paper as I painted. Clearly time to pack up the paints, go inside the tent, and warm up.

The next morning, I awoke to frost on the tent. With the cold dampness of the previous night, water had seeped underneath the tent, and my equipment now lay soaked with water. As I peeked out of the tent, I saw the surrounding hills and mountains dusted with snow, and snow was falling up the valley. Darn, the air was cold! Reluctantly, I left the comfort of the tent for breakfast.

The morning cereal of tsampa, made from barley, needed lots of sugar to make it more palatable. At this altitude, oatmeal was a luxury, and the staple crop of barley provided grain for tsampa. Chapatis, covered with my stash of peanut butter and honey, greatly improved breakfast.

It was after nine when I began hiking up the valley. Quickly, details disappeared as the fog and snow-laden clouds covered the land. The clouds blasted down the valley, and soon I stood in the middle of a snowstorm. Cold, cold, and more cold. I put on my rain pants, my jacket, and my vest, and soon I felt both hot and cold at the same time. As I crossed a turbulent river, I prayed not to slip or fall from the slick, snow-covered bridge. Before continuing up the next mountain, I made a brief stop for tea in the small house on the far side of the bridge.

As the trail climbed farther up the valley, the weather continued to deteriorate. I pushed on through the blizzard, the snow falling heavily around me, affording little visibility. The landscape quickly became a field of black and white, offering no clear distinctions or landmarks, the trail gone from view. Soon, I noticed I could not see our guide, Dende, or anyone else. The world closed tightly around me, revealing only a few feet of visibility directly in front of me. I called out Dende's name, but no one answered. I couldn't see anyone or anything through the blinding snowstorm.

I realized I was alone and could no longer see the trail. I had no idea where it was, nor did I know where I had ventured off from the trail. I was lost, and I had backpacked enough to know this was not a good sign, not a good sign at all. Below freezing temperatures, a blizzard, no sign of the trail, few supplies with me (as most were with the porters), and the lateness of the afternoon compounded the situation. The thought of an evening alone in these conditions offered no comfort.

I found shelter by crouching down behind a large boulder, which offered some relief from the heavy snow and fierce winds. I took out a small bag of cashew nuts from my pack and tried to remain calm as I thought about my options: stay put and hope someone would come looking for me, or move on—but in which direction? I decided to sit down and rest for a bit, until I could think more clearly and come up with a better plan.

The Sherpas carried both my tent and sleeping bag. When had I last seen them? It was unclear, and I didn't have a good sense of how much time had elapsed since I had seen someone. Every few minutes, I climbed out from behind the boulder and shouted Dende's name. As my cry disappeared in the wind, I retreated back behind the boulder. With the wind ripping around me, it seemed quite futile, but I didn't know what else to do. I looked at my watch. I'd been lost in the mountains before and I found it quite helpful to note the time, as it had a way of quickly becoming distorted when one was lost. Without the reference of a watch, I wouldn't know for sure if twenty minutes had passed, or one hour, or three hours.

After crouching behind the rock, coming out to shout every few minutes, and eating some nuts, my watch showed twenty minutes had passed. Then twenty-five, thirty. It required a supreme effort to remain calm. At last I heard an answer to my shouts, but I couldn't see anyone approaching in the white landscape. Slowly, a speck of dark gray appeared farther down the slope and a lone figure slowly emerged out of the snowstorm. As I strained my eyes to see, I made out the form of Dende, a small smudge of a figure in the howling blizzard. I let out a sigh of relief, no longer alone.

Dende told me the trail had forked awhile back and I had not seen the split. When I hadn't arrived at the next teahouse, he had decided to retrace his steps looking for me. I asked Dende how long he had walked to find me, and he replied for about an hour. We proceeded down the trail, walking very slowly and not talking. Short of breath, I rested often. By the time we reached Lobuche, the next teahouse, my body was exhausted and numb from the cold. I stumbled into the teahouse and sat for a long time, drinking multiple cups of tea, my hands tightly clasped around the warm cup. Food lay on the table but I couldn't eat, wanting only the steaming hot tea.

Eventually, I set up the tent outside and wrapped myself inside my sleeping bag to get warm. Too tired to talk to anyone, I wished someone were there to comfort me. My body was beyond exhausted. The fear of potentially being lost in the blizzard had taken its toll on me and I just lay in my tent, resting, and ever so slowly I began warming up.

Dende arrived at the tent with an herb that he had gathered near the tea house. He said it provided relief from headaches. It looked and smelled like the herb I recognized from home called Yerba Santa, though its leaves were much smaller, perhaps because of the high altitude. Soon I drifted in and out of a restless night of sleep.

I awoke at just after five in the morning. The moon was still out, but the first color, a pale, washed-out yellow gray, entered the sky as the sun began to rise. A clear morning, the warmth dramatically increased as the rays of sunlight struck the tent. I had felt warm last night, having slept in my down parka, inside my down bag. A million stars covered the night sky before the moon rose at eight. Orion shone brightly in the night sky, even with the moon hanging close by. All else faded away as the fog came in, but by morning it had retreated again.

I hardly slept, as just as I was about to fall asleep, my breathing stopped and I gasped for a deep breath. This unsettling rhythm continued until morning, a bit unnerving, but otherwise I felt fine. The view from the tent still captivated me. I could see Nuptse, Kanteka, Thamserka, Taboche, Lobuche West, and Lobuche East. Nuptse seemed so close, as though if I just reached my hand out, I could touch its steep slopes. Now, at 16,175 feet, Nuptse rose majestically in front of me to 25,791 feet. The Lhotse-Nuptse Wall extended across the landscape like a dam, reaching hundreds of miles to each side. I continued hiking toward it, wondering how the trail maneuvered around the wall, which appeared impenetrable.

On subsequent backpacking trips in the Eastern Sierras of California, I recalled the Lhotse-Nuptse Wall. Similarly, the eastern side of the Sierra range continued in an unbroken wall for close to 150 miles. The Sierras didn't have the width of the Himalayas, but from the high eastern plain of California, the view was reminiscent of the mountains of Nepal. Well-known to the movie crews of Hollywood, these mountains were often used as the backdrop for films set in the days of British Colonial India, with the high peak of Mount Whitney and the silhouette of the surrounding mountains rising in the distance to be found in several old films set in the foothills of the Himalayas.

By now, the landscape lacked all vegetation. I had reached the high mountains, and the trail was loose rocks, difficult to distinguish from the rocks that were not part of the trail. I walked slowly toward Gorak Shep, the next stop. Gorak Shep couldn't really be called a village, as there was only one lone hut that sat amidst the stone landscape. More of an outpost, no permanent settlements existed above Lobuche, only seasonal ones kept open for the stream of trekkers and climbers. The locals had no reason to live at the high altitudes, in this barren landscape, throughout the year, where they could not cultivate crops or raise livestock. They remained only to man the tea houses during the trekking season.

It is difficult to describe the feeling of walking at this altitude. Everything seemed to slow down. I became more and more conscious of my breathing; like a constant companion, always with me, nudging me along. Although I had meditated for years with some awareness of my breath, I never bothered to notice how many breaths I needed for one step, or rather how many steps I could take with one breath. Breathing happened without me giving it much thought. Now, the constant effort of every breath required my full attention.

As wide as I opened my mouth, I could not press enough oxygen into my lungs. Each breath wanted to capture more air, but there wasn't enough. Breathing still occurred of its own accord, except that one night at Gorak Shep, when my heart skipped beats.

As I walked, I took a breath and began to take a step. I noticed I did not have enough air to complete one step. I needed to take another breath—two breaths for one step. And thus, hiking continued at a snail's pace as I moved closer and closer to Gorekshep.

Part of the reason it was important to begin the trek at a lower elevation, rather than fly into Namche, was to give the body a chance to build up more hemoglobin, the carrier of oxygen in the body. The body required at least two weeks to produce more hemoglobin. Thus, by taking two weeks or more to reach the higher elevations, our bodies could increase the hemoglobin, allowing the blood to carry more oxygen. Since the Sherpas lived at high altitudes, their bodies were more efficient in carrying the limited available oxygen. Thus they were not near as tired as we were. I did not understand how this worked, but I was thankful I had hiked so many miles before arriving in the high country.

The trail passed along the Khumbu Icefall and climbed through the terminal moraine. Little vegetation had grown since Thyangboche, the landscape reduced to black and white and many shades of gray. Any firewood locals needed was hauled up from Thyangboche.

As I approached Gorak Shep, I felt a clear sense of arrival, and at the same time, a sense of completion.

I hiked into a large bowl, a huge, impassable wall rising in front of me. I could see the slopes of China less than one mile away. Despite the bareness of the landscape, a purity and a clarity pervaded the place. The land lay exposed, raw, harsh, continually worn away as the wind ripped across the mountains, sparing nothing as it stripped and polished the land.

As usual, I arrived last in Gorak Shep. Paul usually took the first camping site, setting up his tent a good distance from us, not exactly unfriendly, but rather with that formidable and stoic singularity about him. Sidny and Peyton arrived next and sometime later, I struggled into camp.

That day, Santa looked out for me. He cleared large rocks away to eke out a small spot for my tent. I collapsed into a spot of sunlight, the warm sunshine pouring over me. I felt like a cat comfortably curled up in a sunny pool of warmth on a rug. As I lay in the tent, the sun had sunk over the nearby hill by three in the afternoon, a lovely sight while it lasted.

Once the sun set, the temperature quickly plummeted and the colors returned to shades of gray, black, and white. I got up for a simple dinner of noodles and immediately retreated back into my sleeping bag for warmth. I knew a cold night lay ahead as the skies cleared and a million stars sparkled overhead. I took a sleeping pill and managed my first good night's sleep in days, not awakening until five the next morning. Upon waking, I noticed the plastic canteen of water inside the tent was frozen solid. For years to come, I would luxuriate in the warmth of heat easily generated by simply turning up the thermostat, or snuggling under a pile of thick down comforters. Upon my return to the United States months later, I went directly to the local J. C. Penny store and purchased a queen-size heated blanket.

From Gorak Shep, there was nowhere to go but up. I began the slow walk up to Kala Patthar, a mountain rubble of stone rising from the ground. Despite the slow hiking, I felt great as I continued up the trail, spellbound by the magnificence and grandeur of my surroundings. The trail crossed a large plain, with the Khumbu Icefall to one side, and the mountains, all of them, standing at attention along the sides. I could see right into China, which lay directly before me. It took hours for me to climb the Patthar, and after resting at the summit, I sailed down the mountain in just thirty minutes. Sitting near the tent, I ate lunch in the last bit of sunshine, which disappeared behind the surrounding hills by two thirty in the afternoon.

By the time we got to the higher altitudes, I craved a treat, the taste of sweetness. A few days earlier I had bought a coveted chocolate bar for some ridiculous price at a trailside hut. Ripping open the foil wrapping, I was shocked and disappointed to find it filled with maggots. I could only wonder how long it had sat on the shelf awaiting a purchaser. No treats today. Instead, it began to snow, and the dampness settled into my bones as I dove back into my sleeping bag for a long, cold night.

The next day, I awoke to bad weather. With no visibility, the snow fell in large, loose flakes from the hidden heights. Despite this, I set out toward Everest Base Camp. How could I not, as I had come so far?

I walked slowly and with difficulty. The landscape was very different than yesterday's hike up Kala Patthar. Before me extended a field of rocks and ice, making the path difficult to distinguish from the rest of the landscape. Everything was reduced to black and white as I proceeded up the valley floor toward the wall of mountains, stopping at Nuptse Base Camp. A French team attempted the climb up Nuptse. I peered through the binoculars and saw Camp Two and Camp Four, tiny black specks on the edge of what looked like small ledges of snow. I was grateful that I stood far below them, my feet on solid ground. I possessed no desire to be perched on those narrow specks of snow, hanging on as though about to tumble below, straddled up the side of a very steep mountain.

∾

I HAD FALLEN IN love with backpacking, and more particularly the high altitudes, on my first trip to the California Sierra Mountains at age sixteen. Through some school friends, I heard about an eight-day backpacking trip sponsored by a local church group. I vividly remember the sixty-four-mile trek through the grandeur of the High Sierras. One night a foot or more of snow fell, a thrilling experience despite my flimsy tube tent. A bright orange tube of plastic with a rope pulled through its length, the plastic tent stretched between two trees. Several rocks at both ends of the plastic tube created a triangular sleeping space, the ends closed off with clothes pins to ward off wind and snow, and perhaps animals. I purchased a pair of basic hiking boots at the local Sears Roebuck store for thirteen dollars. It seemed so simple then: pre-Gore-Tex, pre-college, pre-most of my life, and yet it worked surprisingly well.

Since that first summer trip, I backpacked throughout the Pacific Northwest. I worked in Alaska taking kids out backpacking, canoeing, and hiking, spending weeks at a time in Mount McKinley wilderness.

I had fallen in love with the mountains, cherishing the wide open, wild spaces, those spaces not yet tamed. They offered me vast quantities of peace, truth, and solitude.

Later, on an extended break from college, I traveled through Mexico to Central and South America for a year, stopping to hike the Inca Trail to Machu Picchu in Peru. I began the Inca Trail by taking a local train, disembarking at mile thirty-five, or maybe it was mile fifty-one, somewhere in the middle of the high Altiplano, with no villages or towns in sight. The conductor brought the train to a stop, and I hopped off with my sky blue Jansport backpack and began walking, alone on the trail.

The first day of that trek, all of my food was stolen. Fortunately, or maybe unfortunately, this was not a problem, as I became so sick I couldn't eat for the rest of the long journey. The weight fell off my body, and when I returned to the town of Cusco, I hired a tailor to take my pants in four inches. My sister once told me that I had so many adventures and magical experiences when I traveled. I didn't try to create them. Rather, it just seemed that mishaps, or rather adventures, were part of the unpredictability of the places to which I ventured. I did what I could, but like most of life, so much of it was simply out of my control. Years later, before leaving for Sumatra, a good friend of mine familiar with my travels to remote areas begged me to stay in "nice" places. I hesitated, before replying that I would try, as I knew that sometimes little choice existed if one wanted to venture far from civilization.

∾

I CONTINUED UP THE trail toward Everest Base Camp, at an altitude of 17,598 feet. I passed many yaks, perhaps seventy, loaded with gear from the Dutch expedition as they descended down the mountain single file. Many expeditions were currently taking place, including ones by the Dutch, French, New Zealanders, Americans, and the Nepal Police. As I left the Dutch group behind me, they quickly disappeared, becoming small specks on the trail against the barren land.

The hike to Base Camp proved more interesting than I had expected, erroneously thinking that the monochromatic landscape would not excite my curiosity. Instead, I passed huge sculptures of ice mountains breaking through the surface of the glacial moraine. Like tall ice buildings of bizarre shapes, they surrounded me on all sides. I continued through the dramatic landscape, carefully stepping on the metal rungs of horizontal ladders, which lay between small crevasses in the moraine. I didn't feel very comfortable crossing these ladders, but I just steadied myself and moved slowly along, pushing toward Base Camp.

As we approached Everest Base Camp, it resembled a small village of brightly colored tents spread across the land. We wandered among the tents and the men of the American group greeted us, graciously inviting us inside for tea. We knew this was a privilege, and despite our empty stomachs, we knew enough not to eat more than one biscuit, as food was such a premium at this altitude. The Americans had camped at the base for weeks, and supplies had been slowly hauled up the trail by teams of yaks and Sherpas.

Unfamiliar with the details involved in climbing a mountain like Everest, I observed the process. One didn't simply ascend up the mountain, climbing higher every day. Rather, multiple base camps were established en route with supplies dropped off at each location. The climbers hauled the supplies up the mountain to the various camps. Thus, rather than climbing the mountain once, the climbers ascended the mountain countless times as they stashed food and supplies at each camp along the way. This shortened the climb into manageable pieces and created safety nets should the climbers be forced to spend a week or more in one of the camps, unable to ascend or descend due to inclement weather. With the unpredictability of mountain weather, storing enough supplies at each camp ensured the survival of the group, or at least strengthened the odds.

At Base Camp, we met two men from the American team, Gary Neptune, of Neptune Mountaineering in Boulder, Colorado, and David Breashears, the team's filmmaker, from Boston. They told us the third man, Dick Bass, the originator of the climb, was "up on the mountain." From a wealthy Texas family, Dick had developed and owned Snowbird Ski Resort in Utah, among many other ventures.

As we enjoyed our tea in the large tent, Dick came roaring in, bursting with energy, and wearing running shorts with thermals underneath and a long-sleeve top base layer. Dick told us about how the trip had come together for them. He said that when he had turned fifty, he had decided he wanted to climb the highest peak on each of the seven continents—quite an ambitious goal, as he had not climbed or mountaineered before. But with decades as a successful businessman, Dick possessed both the resources and determination to pull off such a plan. He teamed up with Gary and Dave, who each brought their own set of skills and expertise to the expedition.

I think Dick mentioned that after Everest, only one peak remained, the highest mountain in Antarctica. That was to be the seventh. In the States, years later, I was excited to see Dick's book about his adventures, *Seven Summits*, displayed in bookstores.

Before heading back to our camp, Dick graciously invited us to visit Snowbird Ski Resort, where, upon our return to the United States, he would provide us with complimentary lift tickets. One of my few regrets in life was that I did not take him up on this offer, but I later heard that Paul went skiing at Snowbird. Little did I know that decades later, Alta/Snowbird Ski Resort would become a yearly destination for me.

∽

ANOTHER COLD NIGHT IN Gorekshep, with clear skies continuing the next day as I began the return descent down the mountains, eventually leading back to Kathmandu. Every few steps I turned back to look at the mountains, encircling the space and majestically forming an arc behind me. The view was breathtaking and I didn't want to leave, nor was I ready to relinquish the mountain's strong hold on me.

To further extend the trip, I decided to detour to the tiny village of Gokyo on the way down. Drawn by the name, speaking to me across time and space, I didn't resist. Not knowing anything specific about Gokyo, I knew I needed to go there. It involved a detour off the main trail, up another river system, to a different part of the mountain range. I mentioned this idea to Paul, and he too was keen to make the journey.

Sidny and Peyton had other ideas. A rift had developed in our group ever since Sidny had met a man she wanted to stay with in Lobuche. This romantic entanglement caused a tremendous scene with the porters, I think because it was not a situation with which they were familiar. Sidny and her boyfriend openly pursued their relationship, and the Sherpas were not accustomed to this public display of romantic behavior. I noticed it created tension for both the Sherpas and us. The situation climaxed as we descended to Pheriche, where we left Sidny, while Paul, Peyton, and I continued our journey toward Gokyo. None of the porters would go with Sidny, and we left her, as she decided to hike alone with her new partner into the surrounding mountains.

As I passed Pheriche, I felt a welcome relief that there was no blizzard, as I had experienced on the ascent. I continued on to Warsho, six miles down the valley. That night, sitting near the tent, I sketched a drawing with three dots representing the huts of Gorak Shep, Lobuche, and Pheriche. I drew large circles around each dot with arrows to each of the mountains that could be seen from that place. Extending from Gorak Shep, I drew arrows to

Pumori, Lingrere, Khumbutse (in China), Everest, Nuptse, and far down the valley to Thamserku and Kanteka. From Lobuche, I drew arrows to Lobuche West, Lobuche East, Jobo Lhotsthan, Taweche, Kanteka, Ama Dablan, and back to Nuptse and Lhotse. From Pheriche, arrows extended to Taweche, Thamserku, Kanteka, and Ama Dablan. So many mountains, so much sky, and so much space: a precious sight that I never tired of looking at.

From Warsho, we got a late start at ten thirty in the morning, with the skies once again perfectly clear. Paul and I settled finances with Peyton as she decided to return to Thyangboche, and we headed off with the porters to Gokyo, with our first night at Phortse. I stopped for lunch at the monastery at Pengboche. By now, the fog had arrived, covering up views of the mountains. My attention focused on the trail before me, following closely along a steep cliff. I hunkered down, careful to watch my step among the coarse rocks, and continued on the path.

The night in Phortse was warm, at least in comparison to Gorekshep. In the morning, Paul and I headed out toward the village of Phanga. Though it was the twenty-fourth day of the trek, the days passed without reference to a calendar. Rather, the passage of time was noted by the return to the birch trees and rhododendrons, the last bronze leaves clinging to the birch before they were blown from the trees. A golden carpet of leaves thickly covered the ground as we continued hiking.

Once again the trail climbed uphill, and I stopped for lunch in Dole before heading farther up into the mountains. The Dudh Kosi River raged below, and the village of Phanga sat on a plateau, high above the river. By two in the afternoon, the fog returned. The weather cooled and the difficult climb continued. I had done it again, climbed from 12,595 feet back up to 14,925 feet. As usual, in late afternoon I arrived exhausted and simply collapsed in my tent, too tired to move. Yet, I also felt happy as I had returned to the high elevations and, with that, my mind sparkled with the untarnished clarity of the mountain air. Years later, I was hiking in the High Sierras of California and I got a big laugh as I noticed a hiker approaching, his T-shirt blazened with "Life begins above 10,000 feet" across the front.

After a couple of hours, I gathered enough strength to eat dinner. Dende had prepared a simple dish of soup and noodles, but after eating only a few bites I returned to my sleeping bag. I had seen hardly anyone on the trail, and later I learned this trail had not yet become popular with trekkers. With the spectacular scenery, I knew it would not be a secret for much longer.

The following day, Paul headed up the trail for an early start as I basked for a few more moments in the morning light. As I left Phanga, I proceeded up a beautiful set of waterfalls. I soon realized I was walking up the middle of a waterfall, half-frozen beneath my boots. As I carefully stepped over a lovely world of blue and white crystals, I could see the water flowing underneath a thin layer of ice, moving along, searching for an ice-free route. Looking up, I saw the range of mountains popping into view over the summit as I continued to climb higher, reaching an elevation of 15,580 feet, a height similar to the village of Lobuche on the Everest side.

The giant mountains enveloped me, with Cho Oyu, at 26,906 feet, looming straight ahead. As I reached the top of the frozen waterfall, the most amazing sight of opaque turquoise lakes, opal jewels set among the roof of the world, greeted me. It marked the gateway to the high plateau holding Gokyo, and three lakes spread out before me, like three turquoise stones amidst a bed of brown dust.

Various minerals poured into the lakes from the surrounding glaciers creating the turquoise color. The minerals gave them a flat, opaque appearance, as though sheets of bright blue craft paper had been stuck across the landscape. No trees, only rocks and the lake, with colors of deep sienna, aqua, and the brilliance of the blinding snow against the cobalt sky arching overhead. A lone duck swam on the lake, a solitary sentinel of the mountain landscape. Three hours passed before I reached the few scattered huts of Gokyo, the camp for the night. With the sun hidden behind the afternoon clouds, I longed for shelter from the relentless wind in Gokyo, but found none.

I climbed the last few miles with the porters. We struggled with bits and pieces of conversation, in which I learned that Santa and Saila were both married and Krishna had three children. I felt they saw me as a bit of an oddity, and I could see it baffled them to see a single woman on this journey.

On the following day, I hiked farther up the valley, crossing the moraine to the next lake. The views opened up to include Nup La in addition to Cho Oyu. Tibet was just on the other side, so very close. I sat in the sun by the lake as I painted a small watercolor of the stone walls, with the azure lake behind. I felt very peaceful in this place, and I felt content, a sense of ease. The stark landscape reminded me of the expansive Alaskan wilderness I had experienced years earlier: wide, open, and raw. Distilled down to its essence, the land held a purity of form. Nothing extra existed in this barren landscape, nothing not scraped clean by the eons of geologic time.

I climbed up the Kala Patthar at Gokyo the next day. My pace slowed to a crawl up the steep climb toward the patthar, rising to 18,514 feet. As I left Gokyo at seven fifteen in the morning, the village of a few scattered huts became smaller and smaller. The lake was an exquisite shade of opalescent blue with the radiant sky opening overhead. At last, I reached the summit and sat there for a long time, drinking up the expansive views. I wanted to hold onto them, to hold them in my memory, just as the landscape held me close.

At last, I could see the full height of Everest, with Nuptse and Mukalu rising in the far distance, and Tibet seemed only a stone's throw away. The valley radiated peace and tranquility, with a wonderful stillness permeating the place. I hiked down slowly, exhausted from the morning climb, yet full of contentment. I enjoyed a restful afternoon relaxing around camp, absorbing the sun, and reading and painting in between taking in the glorious mountain views. The starkness of the landscape matched the lonely black ravens flying high overhead, the air so thin and pure, almost translucent. The view could be seen without filters, in its barest clarity, with a brilliance that shone through all, nothing obscuring the vision.

A few scattered huts, rough-hewn rock walls, and the colors of a painter's palette, payne's gray and raw sienna, splashed over everything. My mind drifted to the writings of Keats, whom I paraphrased with, "that was all there was and that was all that was needed."

After a cold night in Gokyo, I headed back down the mountain toward Phanga. My intention was to return to Dole for the night. The waterfall between Phanga and Gokyo sparkled like a thousand diamonds. I descended down the middle of it, the rocks covered with layers of ice and long icicles. The waterfall became a river, continuing its descent down one side as the trail rose to Phanga on the other. Looking back up the waterfall, the sky opened toward Gokyo, hidden in the mountains like a magical jewel, unknown to the world below.

I sensed the end of the trek approaching. As I knew from backpacking trips at home, a couple days before the trip ended I could feel the pull of a more complicated life reeling me back in, caught within the grip of a strong magnet. With great reluctance, I continued hiking down the path, with my back to Gokyo.

I spent a night in Dole and hiked out of that valley and into the adjoining valley toward Namche. I spotted an eagle and followed it with my binoculars as it circled three times overhead. My odometer had broken somewhere earlier along the trip and now, permanently etched across the face, I read the number, 143 miles.

By the time we reached Namche, Paul could feel the pull of the city and he didn't fight it. Not yet ready to head back down to Kathmandu, I parted with him the next morning and made arrangements for the porter, Dawa, to stay with me as I lingered in Namche one more night. I didn't feel the need to hurry and I grasped for a few more moments in this remarkable landscape, for an opportunity to linger a bit longer before it faded away like a desert mirage.

I hiked to Thame for the day, the trail passing many waterfalls and gentle slopes. I stopped at the monastery in Thame, kept up very nicely with a wonderful stillness about the grounds. It was formidably built right into the solid rock hillside. Dawa knew some Sherpas in Thame and they welcomed us to a lunch of potatoes before we set off back toward Namche, arriving wrapped in a shroud of fog. The hike to Thame took almost six hours round trip. A damp fall day, an Oregonian day, full of the last, brilliant leaves holding onto the trees before their final descent into winter. That night, the last in the high country, a Nepali festival began creating far too much noise for sleep or rest.

We started late the next day, as Dawa could not find the tumpline that Santa said he would leave for Dawa. A tumpline was the long, wide band that rested on the forehead and extended over the load the porters carried on their backs. This was how the porters carried their loads, quite a different system than the way backpacks were slung over the shoulders in the west. Today, like many other customs, the method of the tumpline has disappeared as porters carry their loads, more often than not, in the Western style. I waited as Dawa rigged up an alternative before we could head toward the village of Choplung.

I arrived in Choplung midafternoon and decided to stay in a tiny upstairs room in a small wooden lodge. A Nepali family with three small children managed the lodge, and I sat in the central kitchen area as they prepared a dinner of noodle soup, with rice and vegetables. They offered me traditional Tibetan tea, which I enjoyed as I faded further into the relaxation of the night. Dawa told me that after leaving Karikhola, the day after tomorrow, we would be leaving Sherpa country, so I was thankful to try the tea. The house was noisy with the sounds of children and the business of cooking. It was difficult to breathe and hard to see through the thick smoke as it curled about us. I soon remembered why I slept in the tent, rather than a lodge, on the previous nights, and I vowed to set up the tent the following night.

Day thirty-two and another ten miles, this time descending toward Katmanudu after an attemped breakfast of doughy pancakes. I headed for Karikola, first stopping in the village of Surky for some potatoes and an omelet. A long, grueling day down the mountain, and by the time darkness fell, the town of Karikola remained an hour away.

I stopped at a tea house and waited for the arrival of my porter, Dawa, the former cook on the Everest trek. I set up my tent and went to bed, far too tired to eat dinner. Dawa was not happy carrying my large duffle on his back, as cooks were not considered porters. Apparently he had met some friends on the trail and they had teased him about carrying such a load. As I lay down, I felt nervous he might leave me stranded. Still many days out from Kathmandu, I depended on his help.

The next morning, on the trail by seven thirty, I hiked to the village of Karikola for breakfast. Dawa tried to find a porter to carry the duffle, but he was unsuccessful, so we moved on and he slowly warmed back up to me. I continued on to the village of Manidingma, arriving exhausted again. A meal of noodle soup and roasted corn was followed by rice pudding and later, a cup of potato soup.

The next day I hiked to Junbesi, the town we stopped in for a layover day on the trip up the mountain, weeks earlier. I had completed a total of 190 miles. With rice pudding one of my favorite foods,

I thoroughly enjoyed the leftovers from last night for breakfast, along with an omelet and chapatis.

The troubles between me and Dawa faded into the past as I headed toward the village of Takshinda that contained a cheese factory. I purchased cheese and bread, carefully wrapped for a later meal, and enjoyed a superb lunch of a grilled cheese sandwich, potato cheese soup, and apple crumble for dessert, one of the best meals of the hike.

The terrain began to look familiar as I approached Junbesi around four thirty. I camped in the same place as I had on the way up, leaving the view of the mountains behind me. Earlier, as I had left the cheese factory, I had passed another "window" into the mountains beyond: a splendid, framed view of where I had been, like a doorway to the heavens above. With my back to the towering peaks, I headed toward the valley below.

I hiked to the village of Kenja the following day, another twelve miles, now passing the two hundred mark in total mileage. I noticed many people on the trail, a very different experience than just three weeks ago. The foreign trekkers became more than a trickle as organized groups began the hike toward Everest. I climbed toward the Lamjura Pass, fondly passing a teashop that I remembered from the hike up.

The tiny teashop reminded me of my sister's cabin, a small home nestled in the woods of Northern California. Three weeks ago, the field behind the teahouse had blazed with shades of gold. Now it lay dormant and brown, awaiting the bounty of next year.

I reached the village of Sete, the brilliant pink cosmos flowers of weeks earlier faded and dead. They lay among the brown dirt, their cheerful beauty changed to dust. But the blue-violet gentians still lined the trail, heralding the last remnants of summer. Just like in the California Sierras, they were the last flowers of the short summer season to bloom. From Sete, I descended to Kenja, arriving at five in the afternoon. Another long day of hiking, and one more day closer to Kathmandu.

On the thirty-sixth day, October 29, 1984, I continued on to the village of Shivalaya, exhausted, and climbed into bed by seven in the evening. With only a four-hour hike to Jiri, I knew that tomorrow I would soon be on the bus returning to the bustle of Kathmandu. I spent the night in Jiri so I could catch the morning's four thirty bus, for the twelve-hour, very long, cramped ride.

ॐ

THE HOURS PASSED IN a haze as the bus rumbled toward Kathmandu. The landscape, now familiar to me, whizzed by outside the window as though the bus didn't need any gasoline, the strong pull of the city enough to reign in the bus.

Upon reaching Kathmandu, my first stop was the American Express office to check for mail. A stash of fourteen letters welcomed me. Despite periods of loneliness on the trek, part of me had enjoyed being out of touch with everyone and everything for weeks, something so difficult to achieve today. Without the distractions of day-to-day life, I could more easily immerse myself into a world focused on simplicity, beauty, and peace. For the late afternoon, I indulged in the luxury of reading letters from far away friends, savoring them over and over again as I lingered in their company.

I fled the crowds of Kathmandu, checking six or seven hotels before I found a room in a tiny place next to the Mona Lisa Hotel. I hid out in my room with a warm shower, and reread the stack of letters before I headed out to find a welcomed dinner of eggplant lasagna and chocolate cake. As I walked the narrow, dirt streets of Kathmandu, the Western smells of cooking easily mixed with the savory scents of local food and spices. I felt the routines of the last month slowly fade away as I relaxed into a quiet night, exhausted from weeks of trekking.

Out Again

*A hundred divine epochs would not suffice
to describe all the marvels of the Himalayas.*
—Sanskrit proverb.

THE NEXT DAY, OCTOBER 31, 1986, I awakened to complete chaos. President-elect of India Indira Gandhi had been shot dead by her Sikh body guards in New Delhi. My plan included traveling to India for the next stage of my journey: a few months across the Indian subcontinent. But transportation out of Nepal stood completely still, air flights into India canceled, along with all bus service. I wasn't going anywhere far away—at least not to India.

Unable to adjust to the chaos of Kathmandu, I made plans to return to the mountains, this time heading west to the Annapurna Range. The stillness and peace of the mountains pulled me once again toward their heights, and I was powerless to resist.

On my travels, I had heard about the Annapurna Circuit, as well as the Annapurna Sanctuary, and I decided on the circuit, a trail of 150 miles, which wrapped around the imposing Annapurna massif. I found Dawa in town enjoying the company of his friends. Although he preferred work as a cook, I told Dawa I didn't need a cook on this journey, but I did need a porter. After a brief consideration, he decided work as a porter was better than nothing so he agreed to accompany me in this capacity. Unfortunately, I didn't realize how exhausted my body was, which would soon rise up and rebel, causing me much difficulty over the ensuing weeks and months.

The next few days I spent in Kathmandu, preparing for the upcoming trip. I hungered for the mountains again, and that overshadowed any awareness of my body. I wrote letters to friends, changed out gear, bought supplies, and ate endlessly while staying at another cheap hotel. During the day, I discovered a nice hotel, the Hotel Yak and Yeti, not far from my more cost-effective base. I wandered through their peaceful gardens, hung out by the pool, went for a swim, and enjoyed the sauna, my body slowly melting into a more relaxed state. One evening I met with Paul for a last dinner before he headed to the airport, bound for the States. We said our goodbyes, each parting for the next journey. I didn't know that I wouldn't see him again for over thirty years.

The Annapurna Circuit hike involved about a nineteen-day hike or so, crossing over the Thorong La Pass at 17,769 feet. A small window of time remained open before the snows would begin and the trekking season would abruptly end. Crossing the pass could be difficult or impossible with deep, soft snow on the trail. Such conditions usually lasted from December or January through March. Since I was on my own, with Dawa along as my porter, I decided I would both sleep and take meals in tea houses, thus opting not to pack the tent.

I began in the town of Dumre, about two and one half hours west of Pokhara. Getting to Pokhara meant another long and tiring bus ride from Kathmandu and on to Dumre, a repeat of the grueling bus trip six weeks earlier to Jiri on the Everest side. I left Kathmandu at nine in the morning, the bus heading west for the five-hour trip. In Dumre, I caught a ride in a truck to the village of Bhote Odar, and another three hours passed as I traveled across a rough dirt road.

After the long day of traveling packed among a truckload of Nepali villagers, I arrived in Bhote Odar tired and with a headache. I found a room in a nice lodge for seven rupees, looking forward to being in the high altitudes again, despite my exhaustion. With the clarity and freshness of the mountain air, it seemed easier to breathe and easier to think. Without the bustle of the city, sleep came more easily that night.

The next day, I began the trek of the Annapurna Circuit, leaving the lodge at eight in the morning, hiking across terrain that was flat and open, the mountains rising in the far distance. I hiked through gorgeous and colorful tropical vegetation, stopping to buy oranges in the village of Besisahar. I sat under the shade of a small tree along the trail, slowly savoring several of the ripe fruits. As I hiked on toward Bhulbhule, my legs felt like steel rods: hard, firm, and strong. The temperature was warm, actually hot, and for companionship, a river flowed at my side.

The rice fields stood ready for harvest. They had turned a deep yellowish color, different from the rich green of weeks ago. A month had passed since I had hiked through the rice fields of the east toward Everest—actually, closer to six weeks. The rice, now cut and harvested, lay in beautiful patterns across the ground, some forming star shapes, and others wide, broad fans. The river reflected a rich jade color, like an emerald snake wiggling through the forest. My first impression of this new trek sparkled with the vision of a wide valley, smooth and less rugged than the Khumbu region, less stark. The valley stretched open and embraced the clear, blue, cloudless sky above.

Evening brought an almost-full moon and another good night's sleep. The big dipper hung outside the window of my room, sitting there as big as could be, as though keeping watch on the night sky. The following day I hiked to the village of Jagat, stopping for lunch in Bahundanda. The tropical vegetation continued with numerous banana and papaya trees, and bright poinsettia blooms splashing streaks of red across the landscape. Pumpkins dotted the land as though a field of orange balls awaited a team of young boys for a soccer match. I passed a colony of brilliant yellow butterflies, dozens of them clustered alongside a stream. A white-capped river chat, similar to the ones I saw in the Khumbu, fluttered over the nearby river. The small bird hopped from boulder to boulder, quickly making its way across the water.

After a lunch of fried eggs, cheese, and bread, I continued along the trail to Jagat, arriving as the sun dipped over the distant mountains in late afternoon. I took a room in the only hotel in the village, a small, barren, upstairs room that was cheered up by a tiny balcony on the street side.

On the fourth day, I climbed up and up as the valley narrowed, my legs strong and steady.

They seemed to be on autopilot, powered by their own fuel source. My goal for the day was the village of Dharapani, at an elevation of 6,375 feet. I stopped for a lunch of fried eggs and delicious rice pudding before continuing along the river and up the far side of the canyon. With the vegetation still tropical, the brilliant red flowers of the poinsettia bush danced against the cobalt-blue sky, and oranges were still available at occasional huts beside the trail.

But quickly, this came to an end. At every turn, around every corner, waterfalls cascaded down the valley walls. On one of the steep cliff faces, there were twelve separate falls before the water merged with the river far below. By afternoon, a heavy rain began, tapering down to a drizzle by the time I arrived in Dharapani at four. The night opened with the full moon, casting its light out across the wide valley, obscuring most of the stars with its brilliance.

On the fifth day, I got an early start, before seven thirty, and hiked toward the village of Chame at 8,690 feet. My new routine included heading to the next town for a breakfast of porridge or eggs. As I climbed higher, the mountains came into view and the clear blue skies arched overhead. The trail went through thick, dark forests along the river and continued on to village of Chame. From there, only a short walk remained to the local hot springs.

Even with the faded light, it felt wonderful to lie inside the tiny area of the spring and feel the warmth permeate my body. I sat there for a long time, submerged in the water, as my body slowly softened. I walked slowly into the village and found a small upstairs room in a lodge. Gratefully, I sat down to a welcomed dinner of noodle soup and fried potatoes before calling it a night in this precious place beneath the Himalayan sky.

The next day it was clear and the weather turned cold, a chill hanging in the mountain air. I heard reports of snow farther north at Manang and met travelers returning, unable to cross the Thorong La Pass. In my hurry to leave Kathmandu, I hadn't fully considered that this might happen. I decided to keep moving toward the pass, and if it proved impossible to cross, I could always turn back.

I stayed over the next day in Chame, awakening to clear skies with the moon still out when I rose shortly after five. I could see the mountains again, this time in the soft moonlight that spilled over the peaks. So lovely I felt both happy and lucky to be near them again, like returning to the welcoming embrace of an old friend.

After breakfast I returned to the hot springs to warm my body, but it was soon crowded with the local women doing their laundry. I made my way back to the village, leaving them to their daily chores. By noon the wind picked up, the sun disappeared behind the gathering clouds, and the temperature dropped. Without the sun, the air quickly became cold, and I sensed it wouldn't be warming up until well over the pass.

The next destination was the town of Pisang at 10,633 feet. I hiked through forests of fir, the ground covered with a thick layer of needles and pine cones. Birch trees returned, reminiscent of those near Tengboche, on the Everest side. Snow began to appear on the ground and the landscape became more and more beautiful, accompanied by the increasing cold. I stopped for a cup of tea at a small teahouse beside the trail in lower Pisang, and then continued to Upper Pisang, another thirty minutes up the trail.

Incredible views of Annapurna II came into view as I approached Pisang. The small village built into the hillside consisted of houses made of stone, topped with flat roofs. The roof of one house served as the yard or open area of the house above it, the houses terracing smartly up the hillside. Tiny, narrow alleys wove through the town, creating a maze of wonderful walkways.

I located a lovely room at a lodge and ate a late lunch of potatoes and chapatis.

In the afternoon, a loud roar startled me, a sound I could not immediately identify. The large, muffled sound became louder and louder. And then I saw it. Across the valley on the slopes of Annapurna II, a massive avalanche was underway, huge waves of snow rushing down the mountain.

I stared as the wall of snow crashed down, mesmerized by its sheer size and power, covering everything in its path, resembling a giant tsunami hitting the shore. I had never seen or heard an avalanche before, and felt grateful it was across the valley from me. Like spotting a lone grizzly bear roaming the distant shore of a Montana lake, I preferred to watch the avalanche from the far side of the steep river canyon.

I knew everything in the path of the avalanche would be buried deep, beneath an immense volume of snow. I paused and absorbed what I just witnessed. Within a few moments, the silence returned and the mountain seemed calm again. From the safety of my distant view, I could see no immediate trace of the destruction, only a vast expanse of white silently covered the land.

The terrain before me returned to shades of brown and gray with little greenery as I climbed above ten thousand feet. I often feel I know when I am above ten thousand feet, even with my eyes closed. I can sense it as I breathe. The quality of the air is different, holding a tranquility, a peace, and the power of the mountains palatable within it. I felt the same majestic quality at Gokyo, at Gorak Shep, and at Tengboche.

On the eighth day, I left Upper Pisang and headed toward Manang via the upper route through the village of Barga. The dry, arid region of Manang sits in the rain shadow of the Himalaya, the wet, moisture-heavy monsoon clouds from the south blocked by the high mountains. Snow falls here in the winter and remains on the ground much of the time. The men of this region work as traders and part-time farmers, while the women work as full-time farmers. Living is tough here, the land dry and rocky.

Fighting off the cold winds, I climbed to the village of Ghyaru, a lone outpost of brown stones, perched on the barren landscape. A series of terraces of different levels extended up the valley, as each home was built on top of the one below. I stopped for tea, and the only food available was potatoes. As I ate, I enjoyed the view of Annapurna II and Annapurna III, and the forefront of Annapurna IV. The river valley was far below and an eagle flew close by overhead, its body soaring with the cool mountain breezes. I sat upright and faced the sun, struggling to absorb some of its warmth before moving on.

The next village was Ngawal, at 11,975 feet, similarly situated on a barren hillside, a wash of brown houses stacked atop each other, with flat roofs. The landscape reminded me of the high plains of Bolivia, which I remembered from my travels in South America years earlier: broad swatches of tan, brown, and ochre sprinkled with countless, low stone walls traversing the land. Stones collected from the fields, placed one on top of the other, formed the walls without the use of mortar. Over two hundred varieties of potatoes, the base crop of the high altitudes, filled the terraces.

The trail steeply descended to the village of Barga. In the late afternoon sun, Barga looked like a ghost town. The monastery, up on the hill behind the town, was perhaps five hundred years old, not as active as it had once been. The stone building caught the last light as I passed below and continued on toward Manang, another thirty minutes up the trail. I located a lodge and took a small room on the third floor. I was the only tourist, the only non-local, for the night.

Traditionally, like other houses, the first floor contained the livestock, the second floor the family, and the third floor guests. After the usual evening of complete exhaustion and noodle soup for dinner, I collapsed into bed by six.

I planned a rest day in Manang to help acclimate to the altitude of 11,545 feet. One could fly into Manang but I chose to walk, giving myself the added days to adjust to the altitude. This had worked well on the Everest side, and I wanted to follow the same protocol to avoid any chances of altitude sickness on the Annapurna hike.

Upon awaking, I could see my breath, a sharp crispness permeating the air. Though manageable in the sun, it was best to keep moving. Before heading out for the day, I decided to wash a couple small articles of clothing. A large basin was located in the central area of the village, just outside the hotel. Here the local people came each day to get their water and wash clothes.

As I began to wash out a small, red kerchief against the stone basin, I felt a strange sensation in the water. I felt resistance as I tried to move my hands through the water, as though the water became thicker and thicker. Then I realized small chunks of ice were forming as I beat the kerchief against the stone. My fingers numb, I gave up washing anything, deciding dirty clothes were just fine, and returned to the lodge before hiking back to Barga.

After a pleasant walk to Barga, I visited the five–hundred-year-old monastery I saw the day before. Filled with more than one thousand buddha statues, the monastery also included beautiful tanka paintings. Dawa mentioned his father had painted a few of them, and I didn't know whether to believe him or not. Perhaps it was true.

Paul had given me some photos of a family whom he knew from previous travels to the area years ago. He could only remember that they were from a village before Manang. I asked around in Barga in hopes that I could locate someone who knew them. After a few inquiries, I found a sister of the woman in one of the photos and I left them with her. Amazingly, she didn't seem too surprised by them. I couldn't imagine this sort of thing happened often. Maybe the whole idea of photos was foreign to the people of this remote mountain village. They lived in the present, and perhaps the past memories recorded in photos did not appeal to them.

I hiked back to Manang, where I went in search of supplies. After experiencing the water freezing during my attempt at washing clothes, I decided I needed some warmer clothes for the upcoming mountain pass. I found a small stall with a woman selling sweaters, hats, and mittens. I purchased another thick, locally made wool sweater (now I had two), a rough woolen hat, and coarsely knitted gloves, along with biscuits, muesli, and candles. Manang was the last permanent settlement below the Thorong La Pass, and the last chance to purchase any remaining supplies I might need for the trek.

After the usual dinner of noodle soup, I ran into a friendly Swiss couple that I met days earlier on the trail. They offered me cold medicine for my nagging cough, and I decided to lay over in Manang one more day so I could hike with them over the pass, thankful for the company.

The next day I spent with the Swiss couple, visiting the gompa, where we saw a puja ceremony. Inside, melodic chants were sung, and I met with the lama, offering him the traditional white kata scarf, which he returned to me with his blessings upon leaving. We hiked back to Manang and enjoyed a quiet dinner in the last light of the day.

As I approched Phedi at 14,895 feet, the last camp before the pass, I felt the altitude creeping up on me, especially with the bronchial cough I had developed earlier. Despite my exhaustion, I noticed the stark beauty of my surroundings, the ground laced with streams, partly frozen as water flowed around the ice and icicles clinging to the rocks. I stopped to eat hard-boiled eggs, Tibetan bread, biscuits, and a chocolate bar packed deep in my pack.

I climbed out of Manang at eight in the morning, remembering to send Dawa off by seven. It was important for him to secure us beds in the only lodge in Phedi. Arriving too late would mean no available beds. By the time I arrived at two in the afternoon, I saw other travelers turned away, the beds full. In Phedi, there was no view, simply a trail going up, up, and up, with the imposing stone mountain rising before me.

The Thorong La Pass was located on a trail, which connects the village of Manang in the Manang District to the east, with the temple of Muktinath in the Mustang District to the west. The pass, the highest point on the Annapurna Circuit, marked the abrupt transition from one major Himalayan valley to another. In addition to trekkers, local traders regularly used the pass. The trekkers followed the route counter clockwise, as the west-to-east route proved much more difficult, not allowing them sufficient time for acclimatization.

The classic Annapurna Circuit trek first became accessible to foreign trekkers in 1977, when the Nepalese Government de-restricted the Manang Valley, previously closed on account of its proximity to the Tibetan border. The original trek started from the market town of Dhumre situated on the Kathmandu–Pokhara highway and ended in Pokhara, and took about twenty-three days to complete. This was close to the route I was hiking. Road construction started in the early nineteen eighties, both from Dumre to the north and from Pokhara to the west, and then up the Kali Gandaki River Valley. The road now reaches Chamje on the Marsyangdi River Valley, and all the way to Muktinath on the Kali Gandaki side.

Out of the original twenty-three days, today only five walking days of the trek still remain without a paved road. Most likely a road now circumnavigates the entire Annapurna Massif. In various places, new trails and routes have been marked so the road can be partly avoided. However, the existence of the road totally changed the area, both the appearance and the atmosphere of the villages. The trek of 1986 exists as a moment lost in time, forgotten in the folds of the past.

The Annapurna circuit and Thorong La Pass trek follow ancient paths used as trade routes between Nepal and Tibet. These paths have long facilitated the flow of cultures and religions in this remote and formerly inaccessible region. Today, Tibetan Mahayana Buddhism, Hinduism, and the mysterious Bonpo religion (pre-Buddhist) still coexist and interpenetrate one another in this region, which contains many pilgrimage sites.

The original route combined a wide variety of climate zones, from the tropics to the arctic conditions at the Thorong La Pass, and included a wide cultural variety, from Hindu villages at the low foothills to the Tibetan culture of Himalayan Manang Valley and lower Mustang region. The magnificent mountain scenery along this trek included Annapurna, 26,545 feet, the first 26,000-foot peak in the area to be climbed, the magnificent ice pyramid of Dhaulagiri at 26,794 feet, and Machapuchare (also known as the Fish Tail), at 22,942 feet, considered by many to be the most beautiful mountain in the world.

I slept poorly in the rustic lodge at Phedi. Crowded and noisy, it seemed like the night passed with no rest before the sound of the wake up shout began. A young boy walked the dark halls shouting, "Time to rise." I began hiking by four in the morning, my goal to be over the pass by sunrise to avoid the sun hitting the snow, warming it, and significantly slowing down the pace. Three thousand feet up, cross over the pass, and then over five thousand feet down the other side. Another grueling, very long day.

As I came out of the lodge, I could see tiny lights scattered up the mountain. I realized these sparks were trekkers already on their way, slowly ascending the pass. With my sleepy eyes, I could have mistaken them for stars in the blackened sky, pinpoints of light in the far distance. I began to hike in the moonlight, following the line up the pass. The sky arched overhead with a million stars. I hiked at a snail's pace, many times thinking the top was in sight, but it was only a false summit, and I continued forward.

Before beginning the hike, I asked Dawa to stay within sight of me, as I didn't want to get lost like I had on the Everest side. I didn't realize until part way down the other side of the pass what an immense mistake I had made, one that would haunt me for many years, by requesting him to walk so slowly. As we climbed, he would wait for me on the side of the path, bundled in a tight ball trying to get some warmth, until I arrived. He took my down sleeping bag out of the battered green duffel and wrapped it tightly around himself as he waited for me to catch up. Too exhausted to understand what was happening to Dawa, we continued trudging up the mountain, Dawa waiting at intervals for me to catch up. It required all of my energy to reach the top.

At the summit, I spotted two fellow female travelers resting on a rock. As I approached, they offered me chocolate. One of them had flown into Kathmandu a few days earlier from Switzerland with a very large bag of Swiss chocolates. We sat there a long time, in exhausted silence, devouring the chocolates. I added the few biscuits in my pocket to our sweet breakfast feast.

When I stood atop the pass at eight fifteen, I could look out over the Tibetan high plateau, extending far to the north. My heart ached for Tibet, but that was to have to wait until another time. Unbeknownst to me, the border between Nepal and Tibet opened to foreigners the day after I left Nepal in the fall of 1984.

I descended into the Mustang District, a vast high valley, arid and dry, characterized by battered canyons, colorful stratified rock formations, and a vast, harsh, desert-like appearance. This included one of the north–south trade routes the old salt caravans followed, and my imagination was filled with the exotic tales of exploration and adventure of ancient times. Before me lay an endless winding descent into the arid areas of Lower Mustang, part of the small former Tibetan kingdom Lo, a remote and isolated region of the Nepalese Himalayas.

With a 5,100-foot vertical drop before me, I began the descent. I spotted a tiny hut part way down the mountain and I headed toward it, a miniscule blip far below, on the side of the mountain. The landscape stretched out in endless stone, the path only rocks. As I approached the hut, I saw my porter, Dawa, in a seated position with his feet in a plastic tub of water.

At first I didn't understand what he was doing, and then it slowly came together. He was experiencing the first signs of frostbite, and I later found out that his right toe had frozen. He said his foot burned and I could see the pain as it moved across his worried face. The kind Nepali woman in the tiny hut had provided a small plastic bucket filled with water and epsom salts so Dawa could soak his feet. Unbeknownst to me, by asking Dawa to wait for me to catch up, I caused him to go so slowly that he could not stay warm enough. Meanwhile, I noticed at the pass that my blue wind/rain jacket was lined with a thick layer of ice on the inside. With my two wool sweaters and thermal base layer, I had overheated on the climb up the mountain and the sweat had frozen on the inside of my jacket.

The landscape of the descent differed vastly from that of the approach. Dry, barren, and dusty brown, with no snow-covered mountains to the north. I was now in the rain shadow of the Himalayas, the high-desert plain of Tibet, exhausted, hungry, and with a headache. I headed for the village of Jharkot, an impressive fortress perched on a ridge at 11,850 feet. I found a very dirty lodge with a room, far too exhausted to look any farther. After eating a small bowl of soup, I collapsed into bed.

On the descent, I passed through the sacred site of Muktinath, located in a beautiful grove of poplars. Muktinath, a sacred shrine for both Hindus and Buddhists, was an ancient pilgrimage site mentioned in the Mahabharata (the book of Hindu mythology written about 300 BC), and also a site of Buddhist pilgrimage. The 108 waterspouts near the temple of Muktinath celebrated water as an important part of the ritual purification for Hindus.

Sleeping late the next morning, I arose slowly and ate breakfast before leaving for the village of Kagbeni. The trail descended farther into the desert landscape with no towns in sight. Far away on the distant plain below, I saw a band of dust rising above the surface. Minutes passed before I could discern a large group of people and animals moving across the plain. They slowly approached, like a scene out of *Lawrence of Arabia*: a long line of donkeys decorated with brightly colored bridles and tassels, their men walking beside the animals loaded with the treasures of their caravan. I traveled through time as I watched the procession move across the desert.

Dust gathered as the animals slowly moved on, carrying their burdens north into Tibet in search of trade. The ancient trade routes, heavily used until the Chinese annexation of Tibet in 1950, slowly came back into use. Since ancient times, caravans of pack animals had brought rice up from Nepal's Terai region and lower hills in exchange for salt from the dry lakes on the Tibetan Plateau.

I traversed down to Kagbeni, the northernmost point for trekkers on the west side. Looking to the north, I saw only the barren mountains of Tibet and the large, wide river valley below, with numerous bands of water braided across its surface.

Kagbeni, a strange town, contained many tunnels, providing protection from the fierce and constant winds. Gardens of cabbages and apple trees struggled for their existences on the terraces, and piles of straw were stacked on the rooftops. The wind ripped through town, leaving everything and everyone covered with a thin layer of dust. With no warm or welcoming feeling to the town, just dust, wind, and the barren dry land greeted me. I check into a small lodge, the kitchen below and the guest rooms upstairs. I had a bucket of hot water sent up to the room so I could bathe and soak my feet. It had been cold since Pisang, and my body had not yet thawed out.

The next day, I headed off toward Jomoson, a town farther down the windswept valley. A clear morning, the temperature slowly increased as I descended. But once I arrived in Jomoson, a fierce wind roared up the valley and made walking outside almost unbearable.

I stopped to rest along a stone wall and was horrified by what I saw. Seven porters sat by the wayside, their feet grayish white and bandaged. I sat there trying to figure out what I was looking at when I noticed a young white man carrying a small Nepali on his back, piggy-back style. I watched them as they passed me on the trail and I noticed the soles of the Nepali's feet, dangling at the man's side, were jet black, like two large lumps of charcoal hanging from each leg.

I learned the white man served in the Peace Corps as a volunteer in Jomoson. He was helping a group of Sherpas who yesterday descended off the pass at Tilicho Peak, not far from where I had crossed the mountain. The night before, it had snowed over a foot, maybe two feet on the pass. With the thick accumulation of snow, the group of trekkers was forced to spend the night on the peak. The next morning, at the first possible moment, helicopters flew the tourists to Kathmandu, as many of them suffered frostbite and needed immediate skin grafts. The porters also needed skin grafts, even more so as trekking companies did not provide porters with shoes. The Sherpas hiked barefoot and they had been caught in the snowstorm along with the tourists. But the Sherpas were not flown out. Their lives were considered expendable; the tour companies did not pay to fly them out, only the tourists. Instead, the company officials left them to figure out their own way back, miraculously stumbling into Jomoson a day or two later.

A sad story, yet one I had heard and seen before across the world, in developing countries. Why was it that, at least at this moment in human history, an American life counted more than a Nepali life? A white person more than a non-white person? I didn't have the answer, but I knew it was true. Whether I liked it or not, it existed, and I was not only white, but also had access to the privileges accorded Americans.

I had experienced the privilege of being white before. In Africa, I could walk into any resort, use the extensive facilities, the pool, the gardens, no questions asked, just because of the color of my skin. Hotel staff assumed I was a guest, even if I stayed in cheap hotels and traveled on a shoestring. No one questioned me, no one threw me out.

I thought of the Vietnamese monk Thich Nhat Hanh's quote: "We all shed salty tears and shed red blood. All is one." Why was it so difficult to see this, to know this? Man's cruelty to fellow human beings seems unending. Is it that difficult to be nice, to notice that we are all the same? With so much unnecessary human suffering, sometimes I think it would be best to join another species. If only I could, where would I go?

To live life consciously, and with intention. Most of the time, it seems quite possible to pass through life on cruise control, on autopilot, unaware of how much impact we have on both others and our environment. Every once in awhile, we may be abruptly yanked out of our peaceful bliss and forced to pay close attention or end up flat on the ground.

As a spiritual teacher once commented to me, it is not possible to be completely conscious of the unending pain surrounding us in the world, as it would be too overwhelming. But surely, we can be conscious of others and their pain, or the pain we may cause them. Simple acts of kindness often require so little energy, so little time. I am reminded of Mother Teresa who said, "Not all of us can do great things. But we can do small things with great love."

Years ago, I noticed a friend of mine repeatedly bought large quantities of bottled water at one of the large box stores. It pained me every time I noticed the back of his truck loaded with cases of plastic bottles, destined for some land fill, never to be used again, or perhaps finding their way to the endless plastic island floating in the Pacific.

I showed him one of my brightly colored canteens that I filled with water. I asked if he might like one of them. He hesitated, and I knew he was thinking how to politely decline my offer. I asked if he thought it was too much trouble to fill the bottle with water every time it was empty. His reply, "I guess so." Saddened, I moved on, and he kept buying the plastic water bottles.

∾

JOMOSON WAS BUILT UP against steep cliffs with the river winding its way below. Narrow lanes moved through the town with buildings along each side, offering protection from the constant wind. Between the town and the river, orchards of apple and apricot trees thrived. I continued hiking to the town of Marpha, which I made my home for the night.

By seven thirty the following morning, I returned to the trail hiking toward the village of Tukuche for breakfast. Tukuche used to be an important center for the trade of Nepali grain in exchange for Tibetan salt through the valley of the Thak Khola. Taxes were exacted at Tukuche in the summer months. When the Chinese occupied Tibet, the trade traffic dwindled, and the native people turned their attention south to business ventures around Pokhara. The local people, the Thakali, had prospered in comparison to other areas of Nepal, as evidenced by the schools, water systems, sanitation, and more varied crops of the region.

In Tukuche, I met a group of three Canadians, Trudy, Joanne, and Cliff, along with three Americans, Nick, John, and Ariane. I decided to head out on the trail with them, appreciative of the company as I continued down the valley. I immediately liked the Americans. The three had met years earlier at a small college in Vermont. John was in his third year of medical school, Ariane loved her work as a nurse, and Nick, who had completed his university studies with a degree in Russian Studies, was trying to figure out which way to go in life.

John reminded me a lot of my sister Christina's husband, Kevin: tall, with a large frame, and possessing a great smile that appeared often. Even his laughter and the way John moved his head reminded me of Kevin. Similarly, John also loved the *Three Stooges* comedies of my youth, and I appreciated hearing stories about Moe, Curly, and Larry as the miles passed beneath my boots.

John complemented the more inward nature of Ariane, who possessed a more quiet and reflective temperament. She reminded me of my best friend in college, Perry. Her manners, her dress, her style: they were the same as Perry's. Not seeming to care what others thought of her, Perry moved through life with a grace and independence I appreciated and admired.

Nick struck me as a gentle man, a soul in search of its place in the world, from which it could settle and grow. I empathized with his confusion, adrift in the sea of choice so often available to those from the west. Despite having so much I wanted to share with him, I knew many of life's lessons needed to be learned by oneself. And yet, I still tried, the words coming out in a jumble, as I encouraged him to follow his heart.

I continued across the dry desert landscape, the trail following alongside the river bottom of rounded stones and gravel that surely swelled with the summer rains. I entered a forested area of fir, a welcome return to the land of trees. The majestic mountains came into view with the peaks of Annapurna I, Dhaulagiri, and Nilgiri rising to the heavens. I stopped for lunch in the village of Kalopani and savored local apple pie before I pushed on to Ghasa. The flowers returned, an abundance of geraniums scattered outside the local houses. Beautiful weather with clear, sunny skies accompanied me, but the wind continued fiercely, disturbing the peaceful ambience.

From Ghasa, I hiked to the village of Tatopani. My body felt tired and my hacking cough continued as I pressed forward. I descended into the river valley and returned to a world of poinsettias, banana trees, and tangerine trees, with the terraced fields harvested and laying fallow for winter. At my back, the glorious view of Nilgiri rose to 22,437 feet. By two in the afternoon, I arrived in Tatopani in the usual condition: exhausted and hungry. Tatopani means hot springs, and I headed toward the village after purchasing and eating some delicious, local lemon pie. As I melted into the hot springs, I quickly forgot about my tired body.

Day seventeen involved a long uphill hike from Tatopani to the village of Ghorapani at 9,429 feet. Despite my aching body, the sublime beauty of Dhalagiri impressed me. I toyed with the idea of continuing on to the Annapurna Sanctuary, a trek of another ten to fourteen days or so, but I let that dream fade away with the wind.

The Sanctuary referred to the high basin southwest of Annapurna. The narrow valley between the peaks of Hiunchuli and Machhapuchhre formed the entrance. This remarkable amphitheater was brought to the attention of the Western world by the British Expedition to Machhapuchhre in 1957, and it remains one of the classic Nepali treks.

Just a few more days remained before I would arrive in Pokara, the town that marked the end of the trek. After I said goodbye to the three Canadians in Gorapani, I continued hiking with the three Americans. We got off to a leisurely start by nine thirty in the morning, and hiked to Birethanti, descending to 3,400 feet. I felt I had returned to the tropics, noting the colorful bougainvillea vines climbing up the sides of houses, toward the sky. The huge, puffy white clouds typical of a tropical climate also returned.

As the afternoon waned on, we found rooms in a small lodge in Birethanti and sat out under the thatched roof of the structure as the night fell. It was a quiet evening; I appreciated the company and conversation over a simple dinner. Unfortunately, something I ate didn't agree with me and my stomach ached most of the night.

I hoped for nothing more serious than twenty-four-hour dysentery.

Focused on the end now, I approached the last day of hiking before reaching Pokhara. I could feel the pull of the city again, the pull of the built landscape. The weeks and months of trekking began to fade behind me as I moved closer and closer to Pokhara. I wondered if, like a mirage, they would disappear altogether.

I crossed another suspension bridge in Birethanti. These bridges numbered so many that I had lost count of them. Another rickety suspension bridge over a wide river, the water flowing much more slowly than months ago. We hiked to the village of Naudanda where we stopped for lunch. It became clear we were approaching a larger town as we experienced the first signs of people begging, something not seen earlier on either of the treks, this one or Everest. The views of the lake at Pokhara came into view and we decided to catch a truck, which took even longer than walking as the truck got a flat tire. Tired and cranky by the time we pulled into Pokhara, we found a barely okay hotel, nothing special, and checked in. We ate far too much food, our appetites insatiable, making up for all the times when food was not plentiful. We gorged ourselves unnecessarily and headed directly to bed.

The following day, John, Ariane, Nick, and I boarded the seven o'clock morning bus to Kathmandu. The bus ride surprised me with its comfort, unlike the ride months earlier to Jiri. As the bus slowly pulled out of Pokhara, the long journey of the previous months began to further recede.

When the weather warmed up, we climbed to the top of the bus and spread out across the piles of luggage. A small metal ladder at the rear of the bus provided the driver access for loading bundles onto the roof. As the sun sparkled and the breeze carried us along, we comfortably nestled among the soft luggage and burlap bags of supplies. We each found a small area and dug ourselves in, molding the luggage to our bodies like sand at the beach.

We bought assorted snacks from the young Nepali boys running alongside the road and enjoyed a picnic of momos, oranges, bananas, biscuits, and chocolate we had stashed in our bags as we rode along on the roof of the bus. By now, I'd eaten enough biscuits to last me for decades. The cool breeze provided a sense of freedom as the miles flew by and we neared Kathmandu.

∾

I COULD FEEL AN end approaching, a closure, the pull of home becoming stronger. It was as though an incessant magnet towed me in and I was powerless to resist. My mind considered the idea of continuing to travel, or heading in the direction of home. There was no decision to make. I realized the time had arrived to begin making my way home.

Once in Kathmandu, I took an expensive room at the Star Hotel. I said goodbye to Dawa, this time for good, and we gave each other a hug as we separated. I carried my bag up to the room, settled in, and walked down the street to meet up with John, Nick, and Ariane for dinner at six.

With the arrival of late November, the fall season ended and quickly moved into winter. Crisp, cold days followed. It was no longer time to be in the mountains or on any of the alpine passes. Kathmandu was quiet, and the bustle of the trekkers scurrying down the street from one shop to another, either securing supplies for their journey or dropping off equipment they no longer wanted, had ceased. The town was closing up for the winter, deserted compared to months ago.

The remaining days in Kathmandu revolved around spending time with John, Nick, and Ariane as I made plans for the return journey home. I moved hotels to the Tuche Peak, where I enjoyed the lovely, peaceful gardens surrounding the rooms. My body was completely exhausted, with little energy for anything.

I felt used up and empty, like a discarded garment tossed to the wayside. I didn't know how to restore myself, how to gather energy and bring it inside of me. Except for lying in bed, everything else seemed exceedingly difficult, requiring far too much effort. My cold worsened and turned into bronchitis after the repeated nights in freezing temperatures, combined with the exhausting physical demands of the last weeks and months.

I enjoyed reading more letters from home, which provided me with a burst of brief energy. I made another visit to the medical clinic, which I had stopped at months earlier regarding the malaria poisoning, securing medicine for the worsening cold and cough.

I visited a travel agent in the sleepy Tamal District of Kathmandu and purchased an air ticket home. The thought of continuing travels through

India, Thailand, or China presented no appeal. Filled with many experiences and my senses saturated, the thought of more traveling felt exhausting. I headed for home, purchasing the best air deal via Bangkok, Hong Kong, Tokyo, Honolulu, and on to San Francisco and Sacramento. Enduring many transfers was the price of a cheap ticket. Today, with little patience for the long hours, multiple transfers, and flight discomfort, I prefer flying nonstop.

I spent the next few days wandering around the streets of Kathmandu with John, Nick, and Ariane. We filled our time shopping for gifts for those we had left at home, playing in the sunshine, talking, and eating a lot. Saddened to see them leave, my eyes filled with tears. I said goodbye to John and Nick in the afternoon, and Ariane rode away in a taxi later that day. Before stepping inside the taxi, we exchanged hugs and kisses and Arianne stuffed a pale, blue, folded piece of paper in my hand. She said, "Your haiku," as she stepped into the car. "Enjoy Hawaii and relax," she shouted out the window as the taxi pulled away. She knew better than I how tired and worn I was after months on the trail.

As I stood there and watched the taxi melt into the distant streets, the late afternoon sun boldly struck the ground with orange and crimson colors as the last rays disappeared behind the rooftops.

I opened the small piece of paper, an elegant, thin sheet of writing paper with a fine tooth. Inside, the delicate small print read:

Sylvia

Wild red poinsettias
Serene Crystal peaks
Oh! Cherry blossoms?

Thank you for wandering about my final Kathmandu hours with me.

Ariane

The Pull of Home

*Who has not known a journey to be over and
done before the traveler returns?
The reverse is also true: many a trip continues
long after movement in time and space has ceased."*
—Steinbeck, *Travels with Charley*

I SLOWLY WALKED THE streets of Kathmandu, not
paying much attention to my surroundings. My
thoughts traveled elsewhere, to Ariane on the plane
with John and Nick as they flew to the States, or
back home wandering the Sierras. I missed them
and I missed their companionship. After aimlessly
wandering the city streets, I felt hungry. I entered
a small cafe on the main thoroughfare not far from
my lodging, and ate a dinner of soup and cake,
before heading back to the hotel for a quiet and
reflective evening.

Kathmandu had become very familiar to me, my home base, through which I had passed in and out of for the last three months. The extensive array of sights, sounds, and smells were well known to me, as were the people, the numerous shops, and the traffic horns, all melting together in a chaotic rhythm.

I felt I had been traveling for years, rather than months. Perhaps because my daily routine varied so much from that at home. Waking up, breaking camp, walking, eating a meal, setting up camp, and retiring early to bed. For months, all of this amidst spectacular mountain scenery, hiking past remote mountain villages, unknown to the world of the auto or any form of transportation faster than by foot.

My routine over the next few days took me through the back streets of Kathmandu: reading, shopping, and savoring vast quantities of delicious food. Overwhelmed by the extensive array of food available in Kathmandu, I moved back and forth between lasagna, chocolate cake, bagels with cream cheese, and brownies. I revisited the travel agency and finalized the ticket home, deciding to layover in Hawaii for some rest. I felt exhausted, my body worn out. I walked into a small restaurant on a side street. The music of The Eagles played over the radio and I was transported to the world of America, anywhere but Kathmandu.

I noticed the following saying tacked up on the restaurant wall:

count your life

by smiles

not tears;

count your age

by friends,

not years.

I found it relaxing and it suited my thoughts, though I liked Ariane's haiku better.

The last few days in Kathmandu slowly drifted by. On my wanderings through town, I bought a lovely shawl for mother and a bunch of silk scarves for various gifts. I trekked up to the medical clinic again, in search of some antibiotics as my cough or bronchitis continued to worsen.

On my last day in Kathmandu, I walked out to Balaju Gardens, some rather rundown, forgotten, formal gardens from long ago. A half-hour walk from the hotel, the gardens lacked beauty or even a semblance of care—an abandoned, tacky, and dirty place. A long row of waterspouts spilled into a large, rectangular pool filled with bathers intensely washing themselves and their laundry. Though not inviting, the gardens offered a respite from the busy town streets lined with too many shops, people, noises, cars, cows, and the endless Western music blaring from businesses and homes.

To anyone who has not traveled in Asia, the moment one leaves the comfort of their hotel, the senses are immediately overwhelmed. Not only visually, but also the senses of smell and sound overtake one. The strong pungent smells of exhaust fumes, burning incense, aromatic spices, and the constant odor of people without access to water for bathing mix to form a rich, thick scent that quickly permeates the air and one's nostrils. The cacophony of sounds, the car horns, the loud engines of the buses, music pounding off the walls of the shops, the shouts of the street vendors, and the cries of the small children accompany the ever-present odor.

And then the visual world clamors for attention with the brilliant array of colors in the dress, especially of the women, the cows meandering down the street, the muddy, uneven streets where one needs to pay great attention to every step to avoid tripping, while paying close attention to the traffic of cars, bicycles, people, and cows, dodging for safety between them. It makes the streets of home seem so deserted, devoid of people, strong city smells, and the constant fury of urban sounds.

Stepping off the busy street and into the garden felt like stepping into a sanctuary, a piece of greenery, a peaceful bench under the shade of a tree, and the sound of water splashing from a fountain. Despite the rundown nature of the place, I enjoyed the refuge.

∾

ASIA, AND MORE PARTICULARLY the Himalayas of Nepal, is not for everyone. My eyes saw the majestic peaks, the beauty and grandeur of the mountains, the warm and beautiful Nepali people of the small villages and huts scattered across the highlands. The supreme spirituality within their everyday life, marked by a reverence for all life forms, touched me, as did the compassion stretching out across the landscape as prayer wheels sent out their blessings and colorful prayer flags fluttered across the mountain passes. These captivated me and overshadowed the extreme poverty and harsh living conditions through which I hiked. Amidst the remarkable beauty existed an almost complete lack of basic sanitation and hygiene: no trash collectors, no street cleaners sweeping the quiet lanes and trails, and few of the modern conveniences that most of us have become so dependent on.

A few months after my return to the States, I heard an acquaintance of mine had recently visited Nepal. I was eager to share our experiences over coffee, looking forward to hearing of someone else's magical experience in this amazing place. He told me he left the States, planning to stay in Nepal for one year, but returned within thirty days.

Surprised, I asked him why he returned so early. He replied, "It was so filthy, open sewers in the streets, and trash everywhere. I couldn't stand it." Without immediately replying, I thought for a moment. There was no question that any sort of hygiene was almost nonexistent. One could not drink the water, flick a switch on for electricity, or turn on the heat for warmth. If one wanted to go somewhere, one had to walk. If a medical emergency arose, one's choice was limited to one's knowledge of local herbs and remedies. There were no newspapers, few books, few ready-made things to buy in shops, and an extremely limited variety of local food choices which one mostly grew oneself.

But my eyes had gazed upwards at the lofty peaks, mesmerized by their unending, spectacular beauty and the power and grace that nature held within its presence. That is what I saw. I noticed the trash and the lack of sanitation, but my eyes grazed over these inconveniences, focusing on the nearby beauty, which was always present, always visible. I thought how interesting that two people could experience the same place and perceive such different things. It seemed we had visited different countries and different cultures. He returned bitter and disappointed and I returned peaceful, with overwhelming gratitude for everything I had been given, despite my difficulties.

Shortly after I returned home, I heard a woman speaking about her recent experience transitioning home from two years working with the Peace Corps in a remote African village. As she relayed her experience of shopping in an American supermarket, I could immediately empathize.

She spoke of trying to buy a can of corn, a simple can of corn. As she stood in the grocery aisle, she felt overwhelmed by the choices available. Did she want creamed corn, corn without cream, corn with salt, corn with low sodium, corn without salt, organic corn, the weekly special, baby small kernel corn, or sweet corn? She said she had crumpled to the floor and began crying, unable to decide what to purchase. There were too many choices. Though all she wanted was a can of corn, she left the supermarket empty handed.

When I first went to the supermarket after my return from the Himalayas, I walked around in a daze, unable to absorb the extensive variety and quantity of food. So much of the store wasn't even food. After long minutes of wandering the numerous aisles, I too left the store empty handed.

I returned home, took out a piece of paper, and wrote a list of my activities of the day. They included:

1. Flicked a switch to turn on lights.
2. Drank a glass of water from the tap.
3. Took a shower with running hot water.
4. Drove the car.
5. Telephoned a friend.
6. Opened the fridge to see shelves full of food.
7. Put a load of clothes in the washer and dryer.
8. Went to supermarket.
9. Went to gym.
10. Turned on the heat.

And on and on it went. I glanced over the list and realized that I would have been doing none of these activities in the Himalayas. For the first days and weeks after returning home, I felt straddled between two worlds: one foot firmly planted on the dirt floor of a small hut high in the mountains of Nepal, gazing out at the snow-capped peaks that were so close it seemed I could reach out and touch them. Behind me was a small central hearth heating up an old, battered, metal kettle for water. Nearby was an alcove of two shelves holding a few cups and bowls. No refrigerator, no pantry, no oven, no shower. None of the appliances of my kitchen at home existed in a Nepalese rural home, or the canned goods or frozen goods or dry goods.

The other foot firmly planted in my home in California with all of its conveniences. The transition to life back home slowly unfolded with the passage of the coming weeks and months, during which time I experienced an immense thankfulness for all the daily actions I took for granted, from safe drinking water to a warm home.

∞

As JOHN STEINBECK WROTE in *Travels with Charley*, journeys have their own ending, irrespective of any particular date. The travels may be over weeks before the official ending date, or they may not be. Once they end, it is as though one stepped out of the time and space of that world, and it is almost impossible to step back inside. Perhaps it is like love; when a love ends, not of one's choosing, it is difficult to find that circuitous road back into the heart of the one that had once so ardently loved you.

The journey across the roof of the world came to a close. The curtain dropped and I knew home called. The day passed in airports and planes, or rather the semblance of a very long day, as I moved among time zones. I noticed the variety of people coming and going as I transited from Kathmandu to Bangkok, to Hong Kong, to Tokyo, finally coming to rest in Hawaii.

∾

PROBABLY MORE OUT OF routine than choice, once in Hawaii, I found a place to camp without considering a hotel. My mind was clouded and in a fog from both the jet travel and the abrupt adjustment to the United States. With no desire to be active or to go anywhere, my energy level hovered near empty. After a few days of rainy weather and cold camping, I accepted that I was sick and checked into a hotel.

That first night, I awoke at midnight gasping for air. Still in the throes of sleep, I couldn't breathe. It felt as though a three-hundred-pound person sat on my chest. My immediate thoughts shouted that I was too young to have a heart attack. I quietly lay in bed until morning as waves of fear washed over me, careful not to move, as any movement made breathing excruciating.

Once the sun rose, I slid out of bed on my back and crawled across the floor. I made it to another medical clinic, not far from the hotel. The hands of the wall clock slowly ticked by as I waited in the waiting room, staring blankly at the dingy walls. The usual poster advocated to stop smoking, citing the numerous benefits over time that resulted, the first signs beginning immediately.

Previous experience had taught me that returning home after travels in developing countries could be a tricky venture. Doctors in the United States simply did not have experience with many of the illnesses still common in poor countries. Doctors no longer learned about them in medical school, and if they had, they most likely had never seen any patients with these symptoms or diseases. Basically, they lacked sufficient skills to recognize and identify the illnesses that had long since disappeared from the population in the United States.

Once in the examining room and the doctor learned I had recently returned from three months in the mountains of Nepal, he thought I might have typhoid. He recommended a typhoid shot, warning me side effects may occur, such as upset stomach, vomiting, and flu symptoms. That was exactly what happened for the next couple of days, with little improvement in my condition.

Meanwhile, I couldn't do much of anything. I attempted swimming at the hotel, but couldn't lift my arms above my shoulders, and it just required too much effort to breathe. Too much energy was needed even for walking on the beach, the soft sand making each step a struggle. I found a movie theatre, watched the current shows, and wandered the bookstores to pass the time.

Later I found out I had developed pleurisy, my lungs and heart injured from the continuous hacking cough that had plagued me for weeks, beginning at the start of the Annapurna hike. No magic pills for pleurisy. I was told I just needed to rest for eight to twelve weeks so my body could heal. The days slowly passed in movie theaters and bookstores before I caught the flight back to California.

A few days later, after a late night arrival at the airport, my sister, Christina, surprised me at the gate. She thoughtfully carried a small, brown bag of food for breakfast. One of my friends had let her know I was returning and I most appreciated Christina's gracious gesture, which clearly signaled our difficulties of the previous summer remained firmly in the past. When I asked if she was still angry from the incident months earlier of me almost burning down her cabin, she smiled and simply replied, "People can change." We walked to the car and slowly made the two-hour journey in the hushed darkness toward the foothills of the Sierra Nevadas.

Today, I still wander across far away countries and far away continents; it seems to anchor and inspire me in this amazing world in which I live, and grounds me upon my return home.

Epilogue

D URING A RECENT HIKING trip in Patagonia, Argentina, I found myself thinking a lot about my earlier adventure to the Himalayas. Perhaps it was the long days of hiking against the snow-capped, rugged peaks, or the barren landscapes of stone, rock, and jagged summits. My thoughts kept returning to that time long ago, over thirty years ago, wandering across the roof of the world.

Shortly after I returned home from Patagonia, I purchased a coffee at the local bookstore. As I waited for the order, I turned to the side, and a magazine about twenty feet away on the sales rack caught my attention. I picked up the coffee and walked across the room to the magazine. On the front of the cover, in bright bold type, was printed, "Why Retire: The World's Coolest 87-Year-Old Patroller." I opened the magazine and I was stunned to see a full-page photo and adjoining article about Paul, the same man I had hiked to Everest with over thirty years earlier.

Since Everest, I had lost touch with Paul, and I'm not sure if I'd seen or spoken to him since that last dinner in Kathmandu. I purchased the magazine and wrote him a brief note. I stuck the letter in the mail with a rather vague address, hoping to connect with him again. A couple weeks later, the letter was returned with "insufficient address" stamped across the envelope. I put a little more research into it, obtained a proper address, and resent the letter. Four days later, Paul called.

Like often happens, the years since we last spoke collapsed before me. Conversation flowed easily, and we caught up about where we lived, what work we did, and of course reminisced about the Everest trek.

This time, when I received an offer to come ski at the mountain resort where Paul now patrolled, I didn't hesitate. Soon he would be ninety, and I knew there wasn't time to wait. The next ski season, I enjoyed a delightful week skiing the rugged mountains of the west, and we further caught up on each other's lives.

∾

WHEN NOT ON AN adventure in wild and beautiful places, Sylvia Verange paints, writes, and teaches in Northern California.

Acknowledgments

ONE OF THE BEST parts of this whole process was experiencing the great enthusiasm and support that my agent, publisher, and the entire publishing staff showed from the get go. My terrific agent, Patrick Walsh, believed in the project and he could see the finished book from our first meeting. Always having time to laugh at ourselves in between deadlines was a shared joy. Tyson Cornell, of Rare Bird Publishing, had the clarity, dedication, and focus to also envision the book making the last year a very seamless process indeed. And I would also like to thank the great folks at Rare Bird who shared in the creation of this book. My heartfelt gratitude to all.